# Michael's
## THE NEW GUIDE
# LISBON

GW00706110

# THE NEW GUIDE
# Michael's
## LISBON

Managing Editor
**Michael Shichor**

Series Editor
**Amir Shichor**

*INBAL TRAVEL INFORMATION LTD.*

Inbal Travel Information Ltd.
P.O.Box 1870 Ramat Gan 52117
Israel

The publishers have done their best to ensure the accuracy
and currency of all information contained in this guide;
however, they can accept no responsibility for any errors
and/or inaccuracies found.

**Intl. ISBN 965-288-114-7**


Graphic design: Michel Opatowski
Cover design: Bill Stone
Photography: Yossi Shrem
Photo editor: Claudio Nutkiewicz
Editorial: Sharona Johan, Or Rinat, Lisa Stone
D.T.P.: Irit Bahalul
Maps: Rina Waserman
Printed by Havatzelet Press Ltd.


**Sales in the UK
and Europe:**
Kuperard (London) Ltd.
9 Hampstead West
224 Iverson Road
London NW6 2HL

**Distribution in the UK
and Europe:**
Bailey Distribution Ltd.
Learoyd Road
New Romney
Kent TN28 8X

**U.K. ISBN 1-85733-020-X**

# CONTENTS

## INTRODUCTION

**Part One – The Story of Lisbon**     **13**

History (13), Geography (28), Economy (29), The Cultural Scene (30)

**Part Two – Setting Out**     **35**

When to Come (35), How Long to Stay (36), Documents and Customs (37), How Much does it Cost? (37), What to Wear (37), How to Get There (38)

**Part Three – Easing the Shock:**     **42**
                **Where have We Landed?**

Urban Transportation (42), Accommodation (45), General Information (49), Tourist Services (50)

## LISBON

# TABLE OF MAPS

# Preface

Lisbon, Portugal's capital, lies near the westernmost point of Europe. Its relatively great distance from Central Europe, and the fact that it is situated on the shores of the Tejo River by the estuary of the Atlantic Ocean, transformed the city into a stepping stone to distant worlds, mysterious and unknown until the 15th century. Since the discovery of these worlds and the potential they pertained, Lisbon has enjoyed a central role as one of Europe's most important bridges to the "New World".

The chronicles of Lisbon, among the oldest of the European cities, are paved with progress and recedence, prosperity and decline. Yet its citizens have always retained a certain modesty and charm. The city's atmosphere and character are unlike any other in the continent, due to a wonderful submergence of many cultures: Spanish, Portuguese and Mediterranean. This special blend of cultures is noticeable in the city's building styles, palace designs and in the rich and colorful cuisine. Even today, when Europe is unified and Portugal is a member of the EEC – processes which brought about a great change to the tempo of the country – Lisbon still maintains her uniqueness.

When visiting Lisbon one should not suffice with just wandering through the alleys of the picturesque Alfama quarter, a look-out from Castelo de São Jorge or with just a glimpse at the royal treasures at Belém. Many sites are located but a short distance from the city as, for example, the palaces at Sintra and Queluz, the shores of Estoril and Cascais and other pastoral towns and fishing villages. An exploration of the areas surrounding Lisbon can be most enjoyable and expand one's knowledge of the country, its colors and aromas.

Much work has been put in by the staff at "Inbal Tourist Information" in order to help the tourist discover an interesting and special Lisbon. I would like to thank all who contributed and persevered  to compile this guide. I am sure that this guide will help make your visit to Lisbon an exciting and eye-opening experience.

Michael Shichor

## Using this Guide

In order to reap maximum benefit from the information in this Guide, we advise the traveller to carefully read the following advice. The facts contained in this book were compiled to help the tourist find his or her way around and to ensure that he enjoys his stay to the upmost.

The Introduction will supply you with details which will help you to make the early decisions and arrangements for your trip. We advise you to carefully review the material, so that you will be more organized and set for your visit. Upon arrival in Lisbon, you will already feel familiar and comfortable with the city, more so than otherwise would have been the case.

The basic guideline in all "MICHAEL'S GUIDE" publications is to survey places in a primarily geographical sequence. The detailed introductory chapters discuss general topics and specific aspects of getting organized. The tour routes, laid out geographically, lead the visitor up and down the city's streets, providing a survey of the sites and calling attention to all those details which deepen one's familiarity with Lisbon, and make a visit there so much more enjoyable.

Since Lisbon is highly esteemed for its cuisine, its wines, shopping and entertainment, we have devoted a special chapter to "Making the most of your stay" in the city. Here you will find a broad range of possibilities to suit your budget, which will help you enjoy your stay.

A concise list of "musts" follows, describing those sites without which a visit to Lisbon is not complete.

The reader will notice that certain facts tend to recur. This is deliberate; it enables the tourist who starts out from a point other than the one we choose, to be no less informed. The result is a flexibility in personal planning.

The rich collection of maps covers the tour routes and special attractions in great detail. Especially prepared for this book, they will certainly add to the efficiency and pleasure of your exploration of Lisbon.

A short chapter is provided on shopping, restaurants, and the other essences of this city. These will help visitors fill their suitcases and stomachs – and empty their wallets – comprehensively, thoroughly, and as economically as possible. Here again, a broad spectrum of possibilities is provided.

To further facilitate the use of this Guide, we have included a detailed index. It includes all the major sites mentioned throughout the book. Consult the index to find something by name and it will refer you to the place where it is mentioned in greatest detail.

Because times and cities are dynamic, an important rule of thumb when travelling, and especially when visiting a city like Lisbon, should be to consult local sources of information. Tourists are liable to encounter certain inaccuracies in this Guide and for these, we apologize.

The producer of a guide of this type assumes a great responsibility: that of presenting the right information in a way which allows for an easy, safe and economical visit. For this purpose, we have included a short questionnaire and will be most grateful for those who will take the time to complete it and send it to us.

Have a pleasant and exciting trip – Bon Voyage!

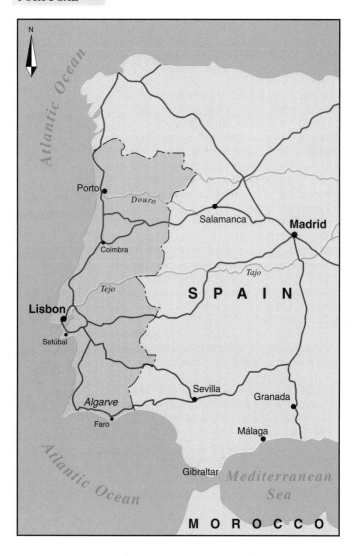

# PART ONE – THE STORY OF LISBON

## History

According to legend, Ulysses anchored on the shores of the Tejo River on his way home to Ithaca. Enticed by the beautiful Calypso, he stayed for seven years and founded a city, until fate beckoned, and he resumed his odyssey back to patient Penelope. Calypso, left pining on the shores, turned herself into a giant snake. The city of Lisbon, they say, is built on the twists and turns of her body.

Historical facts, however, do not lend much evidence to this fantastic legend. Researchers are disputed as to the exact foundation date of the city. Tribesmen of the Neolithic cultures are known to have come here from Andalusia in Spain, thousands of years ago. A wide and calm river, the Tejo was a convenient thoroughfare for traders and treasure-seekers, and the region gradually developed.

A significant milestone in the city's evolution was the arrival of the Phoenicians 3,000 years ago. These seafarers, hailing from Tyre on the eastern shores of the Mediterranean, sailed up the Tejo River in search of metals. On finding copper and tin, they set up a trading-post on the banks of the river.

Next to arrive were the Greeks (6th century BC). They too, came in search of precious metals and the legendary "Land of Gold". Their trade relations with the local tribes helped spread Greek culture throughout the region. The Carthaginians came in the 5th century BC. Yet it was only with the arrival of the Roman legions some centuries later, that the city of Lisbon began to take shape.

INTRODUCTION

## THE ROMANS

Having overcome the stubborn Carthaginians, the Roman legions invaded the Iberian Peninsula in the 3rd century BC. The Lusitanian tribes

*A panoramic view of Lisbon and the Tejo, from the Statue of Cristo Rei*

living in the area, led by the shepherd Viriathus (Virato), launched several uprisings but eventually surrendered to the well-trained and well-armed legions. The independent Lusitanian tribes still have a unique place in Portuguese tradition, having been immortalized as the country's mythological forefathers in the 16th-century epic, *Os Lusíadas*, composed by Portugal's greatest poet, Luís de Camões. The Roman invasion heralds the beginning of Lisbon as we know it today. The city became an important centre in the Roman Empire, and its citizens were recognized as Romans.

Roman rule brought with it a new culture, a new religion, Christianity, as well as innovative methods in agriculture and architecture, including such fundamentals as bricklaying. The Romans introduced a widespread production of wine, improved the roads and the sewerage, and expanded trade by opening new markets and providing safer roads for the merchants.

The Roman era was a time of social, cultural and economic prosperity. During the time of Julius Caesar (60-45 BC) this important and established city became known as *Felicitas Julia*. Latin, spoken by the legions' soldiers, was woven into local dialects, evolving into a new language, Portuguese. Remains of the sturdy Roman fortress built on the São Jorge peak can still be seen today. Other Roman structures, such as the steam baths, and Nero's amphitheatre, can be found throughout the city.

With the gradual decline of the Roman Empire various

*"Lisbon, a capital of Culture"*

barbarian tribes began pushing through the borders of the city: Lisbon was invaded first by the Alani and then by the Germanic Suebi. Stable rule was only regained in the 6th century, with the Visigoths' occupation (585 AD). During this time a network of fortresses, **Cerca Velha**, was constructed around the city. These forts guarded the city until a new religious and cultural wave swept across from Africa in 711.

### THE MOORS

Landing on the shores of Gibraltar in 711, the Moors made their way to Portugal, and, following a series of local battles, conquered the region. Lisbon became a Moslem city, Al-Usbuna. Under Moorish rule the city flourished and prospered, although the Moors left few significant architectural reminders. Islam, which in the eighth century had spread across Portugal, Spain, France

to the west, and through India to the east, brought new concepts of government and architecture, as well as new cultural and scientific ideas. Although Islam became the local religion, Christians and Jews were tolerated in the city. Outside the city, agriculture flourished: advanced systems of irrigation and new species of fruit and vegetables, such as citrus and lettuce, were introduced.

The Alfama quarter's maze of narrow streets and alleys was built by the Moors (although most houses standing today were built centuries later). Major progress was made in the exact sciences. The influence of Moorish astronomy and mathematics can be detected in 15th and 16th century Portuguese shipbuilding. The language has also been influenced by Arabic: many words beginning with "a" were originally from this language, such as the word

*Feira da Ladra (The Thieves' Market) in Alfama*

"alface", meaning lettuce. The Moors ruled the city for over 400 years until their stronghold began to crumble due to internal strife and pressure from their Christian rivals.

## THE CHRISTIAN CONQUEST AND THE FIRST PORTUGUESE KINGS

Many Christians living under Moorish rule in the towns and cities cooperated with the authorities. Other small, remote Christian kingdoms rebelled against the Moorish rule. However, these kingdoms became a force to reckon with only towards the middle of the 12th century, following the Christian victory in the Battle of Ourique. Their leader, the Count Afonso Henriques, who later became king of Portugal, appealed to the Christian kingdoms of Europe to support his holy crusade.

In 1147, English, Flemmish, French and German crusaders joined up with Henriques and laid siege to the city of Lisbon. On August 25, 1147, four months after the siege began, the city surrendered. A large monastery, Mosteiro de São Vicente de Fora, was built on the site where the German and Flemmish forces camped (see "Alfama – A Journey into the Middle Ages"). Afonso Henriques' sovereignty over Portugal was recognized in the Treaty of Zamora as early as 1143, yet he would have to wait until 1179 for Pope Alexander III to recognize his rule before "officially" becoming Portugal's first monarch.

Tension and strife characterized the first days of Portugal's reconquest. To enforce Christianity, attempts were made to remove all hints of Moslem culture from Portugal, including the transformation of mosques into churches. The Catholic church began to establish itself through a series of continuous power struggles with the new monarchy. In the mid-13th century, a century after Lisbon was reconquered, Dom Afonso III made it the capital of Portugal. His heir, Dom Dinis, completed Christianization of the entire country; he made Portuguese the official language and in 1290 established the first Portuguese university (which was later moved to Coimbra).

## THE AVIZ DYNASTY

Tensions between Portugal and the neighboring Castile reached a peak in the mid-14th century when fighting broke out between Afonso IV and his son, Pedro. In January 1355, Afonso IV took advantage of his son's absence from the city to have Pedro's mistress, the Galician lady-in-waiting Inês de Castro, violently murdered. She was forced to watch her four children being killed and then decapitated. Pedro rebelled against his father, and with the latter's death assumed the throne. On his ascension, he had Inês' body exhumed, making her *A Rainha Morta* ("The Dead Queen") of Portugal. All his noblemen and courtiers were made to kiss her decomposed hand and beg her forgiveness. The tragic story of Inês de Castro and Pedro's love for her comprises a famous episode in Camões' *Os Lusíadas* and is the subject of António Ferreira's *Castro*.

*Sé Patriarcal, recovered and restored by Dom Afonso Henriques in the 12th century*

Pedro's son, Fernando I, strove to unite Portugal and Castile. The young prince was defeated in all three attempts to conquer Castile, and was obliged to marry off his daughter, Beatriz, to Juan I of Castile. On Fernando's death in 1383 at the age of thirty-eight, Juan and Beatriz became rulers of Portugal, and Fernando's widow, Leonor, assumed the title of *Regedor* (regent).

Fearing annexation to Castile, the Portuguese began a revolt under João of Aviz, Pedro's bastard son. The *Cortes* (regional parliament) was convened at Coimbra in March 1385 and João was elected king. In August of the same year, Juan I, king of Castile, attempted to invade Portugal. The Castilians were defeated at the Battle of Aljubarrota, from which Juan escaped by the skin of his teeth.

Portugal maintained its independence for the next 200 years. An Anglo-Portuguese treaty was signed at Windsor – "an inviolable, eternal, solid, perpetual and true league of friendship, alliance and union" – consummated by the marriage of João I (João of Aviz) to the refined and well-educated Philippa, daughter of the Duke of Lancaster.

The 15th century saw the flourishing of Portugal as a leading naval power. On a major sea expedition in 1415, João conquered Ceuta (part of present-day Morocco); this was the first time since the crusades that a European state occupied land beyond the borders of the continent. From Ceuta, the Portuguese controlled the Straits of Gibraltar and monitored all ships sailing through them.

One of the more active participants in the conquest of Ceuta was João's son, Henrique o Navegador (Henry the Navigator), who, despite his name, never ventured further than Tangier in Morocco. In 1418, Henrique set up a naval school and geographical institute in

Sagres, where Europe's leading navigators were educated, and expeditions were sent to explore the African coastline. This played an important role in Portugal's becoming a leading colonial power (see "The Great Discoveries").

Manuel I (1495-1521) led Lisbon into the 16th century as a wealthy and powerful city. This was the heyday of Portuguese architecture. The period's elaborate and ornate style came to be known as Manueline, the finest example of which is the **Mosteiro dos Jerónimos** in Belém, built by Manuel I as a token of gratitude to God in celebration of Vasco da Gama's successful voyage to India. Lisbon's growing population of 100,000 and the country's prosperity did not go unnoticed by the neighboring Spanish king.

After Manuel's death, the

*The Monastery of Jerónimos*

Inquisition came to Lisbon. Large crowds gathered in Rossio Square to witness the infamous *autos-da-fé* .

## THE SPANISH CONQUEST AND RESTORATION OF THE PORTUGUESE MONARCHY

According to an old Portuguese saying, nothing good can come from Spain: "We get neither good marriages nor good rain from the Spanish." Portugal's only neighboring country overshadows it in size and strength. This, and a shared bloodstained history, have set up cultural and emo-

*In the Maritime Museum*

*Igreja de Santo António*

tional barriers that exist to this day.

Prior to the Spanish conquest (1580), Portugal had been suffering from economic depression and social çrises. Although trade in the East had brought great wealth, affluency, indifference and widespread corruption also swept the country. Felipe II of Spain took advantage of this instability to invade Portugal without much resistance. He got rid of King Henriques and crowned himself Felipe I of Portugal. Sixty years of Spanish rule was brought to an end in 1640. The Duke of Bragança led the rebellion, and within two weeks ousted the Spanish from Portugal. By December 1, 1640 Portugal was free and the popular Duke was made king of Portugal. João IV, as he was called, was the first in the dynasty to rule Portugal until the monarchy was abolished in the twentieth century.

### THE BRAGANÇA DYNASTY

The second half of the 17th and the beginning of the 18th century was a time of political and economic growth and expansion. As part of the Anglo-Portuguese alliance, Portugal gave Tangier and Bombay as a "dowry" to England. Portugal also began to exploit her numerous colonies around the globe. Gold flowed in from Brazil, ivory from Africa, and precious gems from the Orient. João V (1706-1750) became one of the richest monarchs in the continent. Unfortunately, he squandered his riches as quickly as they came in, particularly on monumental architectural structures such as the Mafra Monastery which he had promised to build if blessed with an heir. As

Portugal became more dependent on external resources, local agriculture and industry became painfully neglected. The Industrial Revolution effecting the rest of Europe was overlooked by the Portuguese. To make matters worse, the dreadful plague that broke out in Lisbon in 1723 killed thousands.

On All Saints' Day (Todos-os-Santos) in 1755 the city was literally shaken. The churches were filled with believers giving thanks to God, when, at 9:40am, the ground began to tremble. Fifteen minutes later the city was a heap of ruins, leaving tens of thousands injured. The earthquake had devastated the city centre, the royal palace on the banks of the river, and other public buildings. The subsequent tidal waves, fires and aftershocks only added to the initial damage. Dom José I and his family, residing at the palace in Belém, were unharmed.

The king appointed one of his ministers, Sebastião de Carvalho e Mello, better known as the Marquês de Pombal, to supervise the reconstruction. With the support of the Portuguese crown, Pombal went to work removing the debris from central Lisbon and rebuilding the city according to plan. Pombal's successful job won him much respect, and he became the king's confidant. The marquis took advantage of the king's passivity to initiate a series of reforms aimed at strengthening Portugal's economy and developing the educational system in the spirit of the Enlightenment. He led a campaign against the Jesuits, limited the rights of the aristocracy and the clergy and abolished laws discriminating against the "New Christians" (Jewish converts). The aristocracy, most vehement in their opposition to Pombal's amendments, had him removed from public office immediately on the death of José I.

In the beginning of the 19th century, Spanish and French forces invaded Lisbon (then with a population of 150,000). After lengthy fighting against Napoleon's forces, the Portuguese triumphed, aided by their English allies. Some twenty years later the battle for the crown between Dom Miguel I and his brother, Pedro IV, escalated into civil war.

Dom Pedro won the War of the Two Brothers, but was mysteriously assassinated some months later.

The following years saw much internal strife within the Portuguese monarchy. As a result many new palaces were constructed outside of the capital city. Social and economic deterioration added to the growing dissociation prevaling between the people and the monarchy. Brazil shook off Portuguese rule. Agriculture, commerce and industry in Portugal remained underdeveloped.

The assassination of Dom Carlos in 1908 in the **Praça do Comércio**, and the military coup of 1910, were the final nails in the coffin of the Portuguese monarchy. After 750 years, it had lost the power to rule its people.

## Twentieth-Century Lisbon

Grave social and economic unrest tainted Portugal's first years as a republic. As part of the Allied Forces in the First World War, Portugal fought a series of naval battles againts its colonial rival, Germany. Social disorder and a shaky economy provided fertile ground for the 1926 military coup. Leadership was transferred from one military general to the next over the following two years, until in April 1928 General Oscar Carmona, a senior military leader, was elected president. As Minister of Finance, Carmona appointed a conservative university professor by the name of António de Oliveira Salazar, who, after setting Portugal's economy on the road to recovery, was appointed Prime Minister (President of the Council) in 1932, a post which he held for

*In the Feira da Ladra, a centuries-old flea market*

the next forty years. At this time, the 1930's, Lisbon had 600,000 inhabitants.

Salazar's conservative rule stifled Portugal and its people. At a time when other European countries were building their industrial and military power, Portugal's industry and commerce were brought to a virtual standstill, not unlike the neighboring Spanish dictatorship. Portugal's dictatorship was however "milder" than Franco's, and was not stained by bloodshed. Salazar, unlike Franco, did not create a personality cult. Portugal remained neutral throughout the Second World War, although Salazar did assist in fleeing refugees and aided the Allies towards the end of the war. After his death in 1968, Dr Marcelo Caetano, the rector of the University of Lisbon, was made President, and continued his predecessor's conservative policies.

The political unrest that continued to prevail in Salazar's time came to a head in 1974, when a military *junta* occupied strategic intersections throughout the capital – among them the **Praça do Comércio** and the large bridge over the Tejo River. The government was quick to surrender. Thus the dictatorship that dragged Portugal into dire social and economic trouble came to an end, leaving it the weakest and poorest nation in western Europe. Portugal's African colonies gradually gained inde-

*In Rua do Comércio, the Baixa*

pendence, and many thousands of colonial settlers returned to a poor and divided motherland. Economic conditions deteriorated further; in a country already much divided, all political parties, including the Communists, wrestled for power. Attempted coups were commonplace and governments rose and fell.

1974 was the turning point in Portugal's gradual rehabilitation. In 1986 the country joined the European Economic Community (EEC). The Social Democrats, led by Aníbal Cavaco Silva, won the 1985 elections, and formed the 16th government since the 1974 revolution. Like governments before them, they too failed to complete their term of office.

Nevertheless, the social democrats managed to recover, and won the 1987 and 1991 elections.

The new industrial areas, modern agricultural methods and an influx of tourists have revitalized the city and contributed to improving the standard of living and quality of life. Massive investments in roads and modern buildings have changed the face of the city within a short time. Today, there are some 2 million people living in Lisbon, most of them in its suburbs.

## The Great Discoveries

By the 15th century Portugal was a colonial power and Lisbon – one of the most important ports and trade centres in Europe. João I's 1415 invasion of Ceuta in Morocco was the beginning of Portugal's expansion and age of exploration. Explorers set out to find trade routes to the rich natural resources of Africa and India (spices, gold, ivory, etc). There were other motives, as well, for these voyages: fighting the Moslems and spreading Christianity, broadening geographical knowledge, and also, giving the nobility something to do...

Prince Henry the Navigator, one of João sons, was the first in his generation to understand the importance of developing the art and science of navigation. As governor of Algarve he established a maritime school at Sagres to train Europe's finest seafarers and cartographers. The annual expeditions sailing from Portuguese shores gradually began to pay off.

A Portuguese fleet reached the Madeira Islands in 1419 and

*The Monument to the Discoveries*

eight years later an expedition landed on the Azores Islands. These islands were colonized and their natural resources – wood, wax, honey, and particularly sugar – were brought to Europe. In 1434 Gil Eanes reached **Cape Bojador** (Cabo Bojador) in Mauritania, then believed to be the end of the world. Eanes' expeditions sailed even further south later, discovering gold. The *caravela*, a lighter and faster ship, was first used in 1440 and enabled the Portuguese explorers to cover greater distances. Expeditions continued to explore the west coast of Africa, and reached the Cape Verde Islands in 1444. On Prince Henrique's death in 1460, Portuguese ships had sailed as far as Sierra Leone.

The thirst for exploration and conquest subsequently died down, but was later revived when João II came to the throne. João II set up a trading-post and a garrison in the Bay of Guinea in 1481, and a year later Diogo Cão reached the mouth of the Congo. Bartolomeu Dias rounded the Cape of Good Hope in 1487, but was forced to return to Lisbon by an uncooperative crew.

One of the age of exploration's leading figures, Christopher Columbus, was deeply involved in Portuguese maritime activity. Based on experience he gained in Genoa and Portugal, Columbus suggested seeking a passage to

*The statue of Prince Henry the Navigator in the Maritime Museum*

India from the west. On João II's refusal, Columbus offered his services to Ferdinand and Isabella of Spain who agreed to finance his voyage. Portugal was thus denied hegemony over land conquered in the west, and for four centuries Spain ruled much of the "New World." Columbus reached Watling Island in the Bahamas in 1492 – later recognized as the first European landing on American shores. On subsequent voyages to the New World, Columbus reached Porto Rico and Jamaica, and later Trinidad and South America.

Conflict between Spain and Portugal over land on the western shores of the Atlantic called for papal intervention and in a bull (*Inter Caetera*) issued in 1493 the Pope arbitrarily divided the New World between Spain and Portugal. The Spanish were to have sway over land to the west of the dividing line, and the Portuguese – to the east. The Portuguese agreed in principle to the division but requested that the line be moved. Spain

agreed, and in 1494 the Treaty of Tordesillas was signed, eventually making Brazil (discovered in 1500 by Pedro Álvares Cabral) a Portuguese colony.

In 1497 Vasco da Gama sailed south from Portugal, continuing Dias' voyage in search of a route to India and her spices. He rounded the Cape of Good Hope and in 1498 reached the city of Calicut on the western shores of the Indian subcontinent. He had paved the way to the spice trade that made the Portuguese monarchy, entitled to a fifth of all profits, the wealthiest in Europe.

By the mid-16th century Portugal had control of most of the world trade. Madagascar was discovered in 1500, and St Helene – two years later. Under Afonso de Albuquerque, the Portuguese governor of India between 1509 and 1515,

Goa in the East Indies was conquered and became a Portuguese base of power and the leading port in the East Indies. Malacca in Malaysia, the passageway between the Indian Ocean and the South China Sea were also conquered, as were the Straits of Hormuz, a strategic position in the Persian Gulf.

In 1519, a Portuguese seafarer sailing under the Spanish flag, Fernão de Magalhães (or Magellan), began a voyage around the world. A year before the three-year journey was completed, Magellan died. Macau, the Portuguese colony in China, was established in 1557. Fortresses and trading-posts were established along the east and west coasts of Africa, in the south Atlantic islands and throughout the Indian Ocean. Portugal now had ports in Mozambique, Zanzibar, Somalia, Kenya, Bahrain, Sumatra, Ceylon,

*Banco Nacional Ultramarino – Lisbon's Maritime Bank*

Japan, China and Brazil, amongst others.

The days of Manuel I (1495-1521) were a golden era for Portugal, and trade with the East, based in Lisbon, brought great wealth to the city. Literature, art, architecture and theatre flourished. Yet, the economic boom, which was not accompanied by a growth in production, brought severe economic and social problems – a permanent deficit, inflation, foreign debts, corruption and sluggishness. Large numbers of people were brought over as cheap manual labour from Africa, and many Portuguese immigrated to the rich colonies in the East.

Portugal maintained a more-or-less steady monopoly on trade routes to the East until the 17th century. Its relations with other countries were ruined with the Spanish conquest (1580-1640); in 1594 ships bearing the flag of Holland, then at war with Spain, were denied entry to Lisbon's port. The Dutch, and subsequently the English, began opening up their own trade routes to the East and other European fleets began to explore the globe.

Portugal gradually lost her trading-posts around the world, and by the twentieth century this previously great colonial power had only a handful of colonies. Goa was annexed to India in 1961, along with other Portuguese strongholds on the Indian subcontinent. Angola, Mozambique and Guinea-Biseu, the last of Portugal's colonies, were granted independence shortly after the 1974 Revolution.

*The statue of Dom João I, conquerer and father of Henry the Navigator*

## Geography

Lisbon lies at the mouth of the Rio Tejo which runs into the Atlantic Ocean. The bay, 20 km long and 11 km wide, is one of the Iberian Peninsula's largest natural ports. From its source in Spain, the river flows for 840 km before reaching Lisbon. Since antiquity, the river has been a convenient and accessible passageway.

Lisbon, or Lisboa to the Portuguese, lies across seven hills and their dividing valleys. Through the ages – fortresses, monasteries and castles have been built on most of the peeks (São Vicente, Santo André, Santa Catarina, São Roque, Castelo, Chagas, Santana). The city's residential area lies on the southeastern slopes sheltering the city from the strong westerly winds. Commercial and industrial centres have sprouted in the valleys. Baixa, the main valley, is the leading commercial area.

Since it is positioned on a geographically sensitive ridge, Lisbon was hit by earthquakes in the 14th and 15th centuries, and by a disastrous earthquake in the 18th century. Following the 1755 earthquake, most of Lisbon's inhabitants moved out of the city centre and into the outlying "suburbs." Of today's two million residents, only 850,000 live in the capital.

Situated in the centre of Portugal, Lisbon lies 300 km from Porto, the capital of the North, and an equal distance from Faro, on the southern shores of the Algrave. Lisbon lies 250 km from the Spanish border at Elvas; 400 km from Seville and over 650 km from Madrid.

The climate is temperate: winters in Lisbon (November-

February) are wet but not freezing; spring and autumn are pleasant with occassional rains; summer is hot and dry, cooled by the breezes blowing off the Atlantic. Temperatures in summer are in the mid-twenties, but occasionally reach the mid-thirties.

## Economy

When democracy returned to Portugal in 1974, the country's leaders were faced with an economy in disrepair. Portugal is still paying the price for having neglected its agriculture and industry, and for having been dependent on colonial trade. The influx of returning colonial repatriates in the 1970s only aggravated the country's already severe economic and social problems.

The dictatorship years (1932-1974) were a time of economic and social stagnation. The socialist government that came to power after the revolution initiated a series of reforms, amongst them nationalization of factories, large companies and vast estates. Social unrest often deteriorated into violent conflicts. Despite continual reshuffling of the government, including coalitions with the right, the situation hardly improved. Unlike Spain which prospered during the 1970's and 80's, Portugal gradually became the poorest and most backward country in western Europe.

Economic dispair was the main reason for the Socialist victory in the 1983 elections; Mário Soares, the party's leader, who formed a coalition with the Social-Democrats, found himself faced with a large national debt and almost 15% unemployment. 60% of Portugal's food supply was being imported due to the unfortunate state of the country's agriculture, while the remaining 40% was being produced domestically by over a quarter (!) of the country's work force, using primitive and unpractical farming methods.

The government set out to cut subsidies, privatize the market, raise taxes and invest in modernization and creating new jobs. Portugal's economy began to recover, not without demonstrations on the right and left. After joining the EEC in 1986, large grants of some $2 billion which began flowing

into the country were put into the development of infrastructure. The economy began to stabilize, but has not soared as in neighboring Spain. Wages are still the lowest in western Europe, although inflation has settled at a steady 12%. Unemployment has dropped to four percent, due to large investments in Portugal's main sources of income – tourism, wine, textiles and shoes. These encouraging figures and an influx of massive German and US investments are signs of hope for the country's economy.

## The Cultural Scene

Literature has always been an important part of Portugal's cultural life, evidenced by the statues of renowned poets, writers and playwrights gracing the city's squares and streets. Primarily because of the language barrier, the works of many Portuguese writers have remained unknown beyond the country's borders. Among the most famous are Gil Vicente, the 15th-century playwright, considered the father of Portuguese theatre; Luís de Camões, a 16th-century poet and patriot whose great epic, *Os Lusíadas*, is considered the richest text in Portuguese; and Fernando Pessoa, Portugal's greatest modern poet who died in 1935. Probably Portugal's most famous and well-loved writer is José Saramago. Born in 1922, Saramago never completed high school, but went on to write a monumental work of literature *The Convent Memorial* (1982). His second novel, *O Evangelho Segundo Jesus Cristo*, published in 1990, caused a government

*In the Calouste Gulbenkian Museum*

scandal. The book sold hundreds of thousands of copies, and was translated into several languages.

Among the better-known artists of Lisbon are the 15th-century court painter, Nuno Gonçalves; Joaquim Machado de Castro, the 18th-century sculptor of José I's statue in Praça do Comércio in central Lisbon; and the modern painter Almada Negreiros. A fund set up by Calouste Gulbenkian, an Armenian oil magnate, finances and encourages many of the capital's cultural activities.

*A shopping centre in Bairro Alto*

Since the 18th century the city's artistic life has been closely associated with the cafés in the Chiado and Rossio areas. Some say Lisbon's artists spend most of their time in the city's cafés and are left with little time to create. A walk through the city's galleries and museums proves otherwise. To get a taste of the country's contemporary art scene, pay a visit to the **Centre of Modern Art** (Centro de Arte Moderna), established by the Gulbenkian fund.

*Fado*, with its Christian, Moorish and popular sources, is probably the most popular musical style in Portugal. Amália Rodrigues, Portugal's best-known singer of fado, has been performing since 1940 and has gained national and international acclaim.

### ARCHITECTURE

Although Lisbon was founded thousands of years ago, most of the buildings you'll see were built after central Lisbon was devastated by the great earthquake of 1755.

From the time of the Christian conquest, the city's builders have taken advantage of the region's unique topography. Palaces, fortresses and monasteries dot the hilltops, and residential and commercial areas line the hill-sides and valleys.

The most impressive buildings are those dating from the Gothic period. One of the finest examples is the Carmo Monastery on the western hills of Lisbon. This architectural style revolutionalized the entire concept of space in architecture, in its attempt to dwarf man's dimensions and glorify

*An azulejo mosaic in the Alfama quarter*

the name of God. Stone walls and high pillars were built to support intricate networks of arches and large balconies. The great earthquake shook the roof of the Carmo Monastery, leaving only the elegant arches that stand to this day.

The Manueline style, named after Manuel I (1495-1521), evolved in Portugal in the 16th century. This ornamental and embellished style is characterized by intricate stone carvings, flamboyant balconies and particularly ornate façades. The Manueline style is also clearly influenced by the Plateresque style common in Spain; the Moors Mudéjar style of the 11th to the 15th centuries; as well as Italian and northern European influences. Christianity (crosses), the military (Manuel I depicted as a great military hero, for

example), and the sea (corals, shells, ropes, sails, etc) are the most common motifs in Manueline decorations. The Monastery of Jerónimos in Belém is clearly the most perfect example of Manueline architecture.

Appointed in charge of the reconstruction of the city centre after the 1755 earthquake, Marquês de Pombal cleaned up the area and rebuilt a network of streets. Baroque-style buildings were constructed and a convenient area for transport and trade developed. This part of the city is often referred to as "Pombaline Lisbon" after its original planner.

Many buildings and streets are decorated with colorful ceramic tiles (*azulejos*), a Moorish "improvement" on Greek and Roman mosaic art. These tiles were first carved and painted on stone, but from the 17th century they began to take on their present shape in Lisbon. Some of the most beautiful tiles are on exhibit at the **Tile Museum** (Museu dos Azulejos) and the Madre de Deus Monastery in the eastern part of the city. A workshop at the Tile Museum demonstrates this ancient ceramic art.

### RELIGION
Christianity, Portugal's national religion, first arrived with the Visigoths in the 6th century. In 1276, Pedro Hispano, a native of Lisbon,

became the first and only Portuguese Pope, Pope João XXI.

The city's patron saint, São Vicente, lived in Spain in the 4th century, and was killed during Diocletian's persecutions of the first Christians. São Vicente's body miraculously reached the shores of Algrave in the 18th century. This part of the country was under Christian rule during the Moslem invasion. When Lisbon was reconquered, São Vicente's remains were brought to the city and he was proclaimed its patron saint. The city's coat of arms displays a ship (which carried São Vicente's body to Portugal) and above it, two crows, believed to have guarded the ship on its journey.

The Catholic Church, for centuries a main axis in political and social matters, owned large pieces of land and had enormous political power. Portuguese monarchs were forced to consider the Church in all decisions made and they generally maintained a close relationship. The Inquisition and the public burnings (*auto-da-fé*) of the 16th century were political as well as religious events. Powerful religious orders, particularly the Jesuits, were "religious armies" spreading their influence across the globe, from Brazil to Japan. There were devout believers at all levels of society, and religious ceremonies were celebrated with great enthusiasm.

The Marquês de Pombal led a bitter war against the Jesuits, banishing them from the country and from their missions in the colonies in 1773. Portugal was the first to take violent action against the Jesuit Society, later followed by the other European countries.

Church and state were separated in the twentieth century. The church still has a strong influence in the rural areas, yet in Lisbon it has stepped down from its traditional posts of power, such as the supervision of marriage. Until recently, only Catholic marriages were endorsed, and divorce was prohibited. Today, civil marriage and divorce are acceptable in Lisbon.

*In the Monastery of Jerónimos*

There is still a strong religious tradition in the country, and miracles, such as the apparition of the Holy Virgin in Fatima, are believed to be proof of God's love for the Portuguese.

## BULLFIGHTING

Portuguese bullfighting (*tourada*), a traditional art and form of entertainment, is a slightly different version to the better-known Spanish *corrida*. The Portuguese corridas are more "moderate." The bull is not killed at the end of the fight, but rather taken to the lush grazing grounds in the country to end its days.

To the sound of the brass band, the event begins with a colourful parade of all participants, including horses in traditional dress. In the *pega à Portugue-sa* the unarmed *toureiro* must get in close to the bull, and bring it to the ground by the horns.

Bullfights are held at the **Praça de Touros** in the city's northern Campo Pequeno quarter. The tourada season opens on the first day of Easter and lasts until the beginning of autumn. Tickets can be purchased at the arena on the day of the fight, or at the ticket booth on Praça dos Restauradores. It's hard to miss the long line to the ticket office on the south-western part of the square. Take the underground (Campo Pequeno Station) or bus no. 1, 21, 32 or 45 from Rossio in the city centre to get to the ring. In the hotter months, it is wise to come equipped with hat, sunglasses and suntan lotion.

*Praça de Touros, the bullfighting arena*

# PART TWO – SETTING OUT

## When to Come

Justifiably called "The California of the Continent," Portugal enjoys pleasant weather all year round. This is due mainly to the moderating effect of the Atlantic Ocean on the climate. Situated in the centre of the country, Lisbon is a convenient starting point to get to the hotter beaches of the Algarve in the south, or to the wetter and slightly colder Porto in the north.

Weather-wise, the best time to visit Lisbon is during spring (April-May) and autumn (September-October) when the temperatures are in the low twenties, although you may be caught in the occasional rain showers. Temperatures in summer can rise into the 30's, but are pleasantly cooled by the west winds coming off the sea.

Rain is unlikely in summer, and even in winter (November to mid-March); although it can be quite damp, temperatures hardly fall below 10ºC.

## Festivals and Holidays

Portugal has two kinds of holidays: official holidays (*feriado obrigad*) and local festivals (*feriado municipais*). Saint Anthony's Day (June 13) is Lisbon's most festive holiday. Balls, parades and firework displays are held throughout the city, and particularly in the Alfama quarter, near the Church of Santo António.

### PUBLIC HOLIDAYS
January 1 – New Year (ano Novo)

February (date changes) – Carnival (Carnaval)

End of March (date changes) – Holy Friday (Santa Sexta-Feira)

April 25 – Liberation Day (Dia da Liberdade), celebrating the 1974 Revolution

May 1 – Labour Day (Dia do Trabalhador)

June – Corpus Christi (Corpo de Deus)

December 1 – Independence Day (Restauração de Independência)

December 8 – Day of Immaculate Conception (Imaculada Conceição)

December 25 – Christmas (Natal)

June 10 – Portugal Day (Dia de Portugal)

June 13 – Saint Anthony's Day (Dia do Santo António)

August 15 – Day of Ascension (Assunção)

October 5 – Republic Day (Implantação da República), since 1910

November 1 – All Saints' Day (Todos-os-Santos)

## How Long to Stay?

The answer, of course, depends on your budget and your plans. You'll need at least three days to see Lisbon's main sites, and perhaps another day or two to take in the scenic landscapes and cultural gems just outside the city (Sintra, Estoril, Cascais, Queluz, Mafra, and others). The pace in Lisbon is somewhat slower than in Europe's other capital cities; to enjoy the layed-back atmos-

phere, it's best not to crowd your days with things to do.

## Documents and Customs

Make sure your passport is valid for the time you'll be spending in Portugal. Student cards, as in most European countries, won't get you large discounts, except for museums, air travel, etc. If you are planning to motor through Portugal, make sure your international driver's license is valid.

Like the rest of Europe, customs allows you to bring in personal equipment (cameras, five films), as well as 200 cigarettes (or 50 cigars), a bottle of wine, and one litre of alcohol.

## How Much does It Cost?

By European standards, Portugal is relatively inexpensive. Prices are cheaper than in Spain. Food, transportation (in and outside of Lisbon), local wines and alcohol are particularly cheap.

Luxury tourism, as it is everywhere else, is expensive here. A five-star hotel with meals at the city's top restaurants can cost around US$400 a night

per couple. Four-star hotels are in the $200-270 range; three and two-star hotels can cost you around $160 per couple, or $100 per single. A night at a local pension, meals at popular restaurants, and sight-seeing on foot shouldn't cost you more than $55 a day. Those who plan on camping and getting their food at the supermarkets can make do, although not in great comfort, with $35 a day.

Car rental rates are much the same as elsewhere in Europe. Small cars can be rented for about $200 a week; larger cars for about $330 (including free mileage, not including gas and taxes). Tickets for fado shows, bullfighting and discotheques are $15 or more, depending on the event. Prices outside of Lisbon are 30% less (except in the Algarve). Transportation is particularly cheap. Museums and botanical gardens charge a small entrance fee.

## What to Wear

There's no need to pack your finest garb for Lisbon. Summer calls for no more than a light, sporty wardrobe. Those planning to spend some time on the beaches in the south should bring bathing suits, hats and suntan lotion. Comfortable walking shoes are a must throughout the year. And you'll need warm clothes and an umbrella for winter. In the spring and fall it is best to have a coat handy, particularly at night. Bring at least one suit or fancy dress if you're planning to attend formal dinners or visit the casino in Estoril.

## How to Get There

### FROM THE AIRPORT

Lisbon's Portela Airport is 11km out of the city. It links the city with several destinations in Europe and America, both through *TAP*, Portugal's national airline, and through most of the international airlines, such as *TWA* and *British Airways*. Updated information regarding flight arrivals and departures can be obtained by Tel. 841 50 00, 841 67 90. There are also charter and package deals, inland flights to Porto and Faro, and flights to the Azores and Madeira Islands.

The airport (*aeroporto*) has a tourist bureau as well as an office through which to reserve hotel accommodation. There are also the usual coffee shops, restaurants, bureaus de change and duty free shops.

There is convenient transport to the city from Portela Airport. The easiest way is to take one of the taxis waiting outside the passenger lounge (be sure the driver turns his meter on!). If your luggage weighs over 30kg you will have to pay an additional 50 percent. A ride into the city should take about 15 minutes; a little longer during rush hours.

The *Green Line* (*Linha Verde*) express bus runs from the airport to the city's international railway station (Santa Apolónia), and is slightly more expensive than the regular bus (nos. 44 and 45). The *Green Line* goes through the city centre and stops at Rossio. *Aero-bus* is a new service, also linking the airport with the city centre. It operates daily between 7am and 9pm, departures every 20 minutes. The tickets are valid for any journey that day on the bus, tram or elevator network (for details call Tel. 363 92 26 or 363 93 43). The regular scheduled buses leaving every 15 minutes during the day, are marked *C. Sodré,* indicating that they go to Cais do Sodré, near the Praça do Comércio in central Lisbon. You will need local currency to buy tickets; take advantage of the bank in the passenger's lounge to change your money before leaving the terminal.

## BY TRAIN

Tourists travelling from western Europe, as well as from Porto and northern Portugal, will arrive at Santa Apolónia station. This large station has several banks, restaurants, newspaper stands, etc. There is a taxi stand outside the station. Praça do Comércio is in walking distance of the station. To get to Rossio take the Green Line that runs between the station and the airport, or one of the regular buses that stop outside the station (no. 3, for example).

*Feira da Ladra flea market*

The numerous holiday-makers coming in from the Algarve beaches in the south will arrive at Barreiro Station, on the south bank of the Tejo River. To cross the river, take the ferry connecting the station to Praça do Comércio. There's a crossing every ten minutes,

*Santa Apolónia Railway Station*

## BY BUS

Various companies provide bus service between Lisbon and the main European cities. Buses, running 24 hours a day, are comfortable and air-conditioned, and drivers change along the way. There are hour long stops at large restaurants along the way for meals. Long-distance journeys can be tiring, and although the bus is cheaper than the train, it also takes longer and is much less comfortable. For example, a bus journey to Paris can take up to 30 hours; by train – 25.

An exception to the rule is the bus trip from southern Spain, Málaga and Seville, which takes only nine hours, whereas a train ride can take up to 24 hours due to geographical obstacles and the need to change trains along the way. Buses run almost daily during the summer tourist season; at other times of the year, two or three times a week. There is also an efficient inter-city bus service to Porto, Faro, Lagos, Coimbra, etc. Prices are more or less the same as the train.

If you're arriving from outside Portugal the bus will bring you to the Rodoviária Nacional terminus on 18 Casal Ribeiro, a 15 minute walk or a short bus-ride from central Lisbon. The station is close to Praça Saldanha. If you wish to travel to the north or south of Portugal you'll find bus agencies on Alfândega Street (southeast off Praça do Comércio).

*Picturesque trams traverse the streets of Lisbon*

and the price is included in your train ticket from the south.

There are two other stations serving those travelling to nearer destinations. From the beautiful Rossio station, trains leave for Queluz and Sintra; from the Cais do Sodré station you can get the popular connection to Belém, Estoril and Cascais. Both these lines run all day. The stations are particularly crowded during rush hours with commuters coming into Lisbon in the morning and travelling back home at the end of the day.

Interrail and Eurail Passes are valid in Portugal. For further information, Tel. 888 40 25.

For information on departure times contact either the *Julia* company for international buses (Tel. 57 17 45) the *Carris* company (Tel. 363 93 43), or the Rodoviária Nacional station (Tel. 54 54 39).

### BY CAR

Trams, one way streets and other "obstacles" make driving in Lisbon an inconvenient and unadvisable experience. Outside the city, on the other hand, car travel is convenient and pleasurable. There is no shortage of gas stations along the main roads.

Some of the main highways in Portugal have toll-booths – not cheap, but the new roadways are excellently marked. The distance between Portugal's large cities is relatively short, and being in the centre of the country, Lisbon is only a few hours drive from other cities. A drive from Porto takes four hours (313km); from Évora – two hours (150km); and from Faro – four hours (300km).

In the city, the speed limit is 60 km/h; outside the city – 90 km/h; and on the freeways – 120 km/h.

For emergencies (police, fire department, ambulance and first aid) call 115. Automobile associations that have agree-ments with the *Portuguese Automobile Club (Club de Automóvel de Portugal)* can get repairs and tow services 24 hours a day – Tel. 57 78 58 or 356 39 31.

*Normal* petrol is low-octane; it is better to fill up with *super*, a higher octane petrol. *Sem Chumbo* is lead-free.

# PART THREE –
# EASING THE SHOCK: WHERE HAVE WE LANDED?

## Urban Transportation

Lisbon's transport service is uniquely efficient. Buses will get you almost anywhere in the city, and there are also trams (*eléctricos*), the Metro, funiculars, and elevators (*elevadores*). Riding the elevators is usually an experience in itself. The tram is generally better than the bus. There are also ferry services connecting the banks of the Tejo River.

**TAXIS**
Black-and-green taxis operate throughout the city, and their rates are of the lowest in Europe, though you will occasionally have to "remind" the driver to turn on his or her meter. Add 20% if taking a taxi at night; 50% if your luggage is over 30kg. There are taxi stations across the city, but not at the main squares. Ringing a taxi will cost you a little more. Note that the rush hour is the hardest time to find a taxi:

*Rádio-Táxis de Lisboa*: Tel. 825 06 19.
*Autocoop*: Tel. 659 15 18.

Taxi drivers will be glad to direct you to the local fado houses, discotheques and other night spots, though since most drivers don't speak any foreign languages, it's best to have your destination written out on a piece of paper.

**BUSES (*AUTOCARROS*)**
Lisbon's buses run at 10-20 minute intervals between 8am and 8pm, and at half-hour intervals early in the morning or late at night.

Single tickets can be bought from the driver. Cheap packages of ten (*caderneta*) are available at the central stations and kiosks. These tickets are valid for the trams as well. Three or seven-day tourist passes (*Passe Turístico*) are good for all innercity transportation. You'll need a passport and photograph to get a pass from the orange and white *Carris* (the public transportation company) stands.

Be sure to have small change handy. Drivers will more often than not tell you they are out of change.

### TRAMS (*ELÉCTRICOS*)
Trams run throughout the city and are a picturesque and convenient way to get up and down the steeper hills. At the end of each journey the driver and his assistant reverse the seats and the electrical connections.

Trams were originally installed in Lisbon by the British in 1901 and the fourteen existing trams were built in England. The Bairro Alto-Castelo-Prazeres route (no. 28) is the most scenic and it is worth staying on until the end of the ride. The stops (*paragem*) are all marked above the tracks, not on the sidewalks, as with buses. Tickets can be bought directly from the driver, or packages of ten at reduced prices can be bought from the kiosk at each stop.

### ELEVATORS (*ELEVADORES*)
Elevators were installed at the turn of the century to help ascend the city's hills. Raoul Mesnier, a French architect and engineer, is responsible for introducing the elevators. The

*Elevador de Santa Justa*

first elevator, **Elevador do Lavra**, was built in 1884; the second, **Elevador do Glória**, was built a year later. In 1892 the **Elevador da Bianca** was installed, and still operates, connecting São Paulo Street with Largo do Calhariz in Bairro Alto. The last elevator to be installed, Elevador de Santa Justa, has connected Baixa to the Bairro Alto quarter since 1902.

The elevators are inexpensive and run between 7am and midnight.

### UNDERGROUND (*METROPOLITANO*)
Lisbon's Metro is new and convenient, although tourists will hardly find it useful, as its two lines don't reach most tourist sites. The Metro operates until midnight. Tickets can be bought at the

*Trams make a convenient vehicle in Lisbon's numerous hills*

entrance to the platform and are 40% cheaper if bought in packages of ten (though this is more than any tourist will need).

The Metro is useful for getting to the Gulbenkian Museum (São Sebastião station), and to the bullfighting ring (Campo Pequeno station), as well as to the Rodoviária central bus station (saldanha station).

### FERRIES (*CARRIERAS FLUVIAIS*)
Six ferries connect the platforms nearest the Praça do Comércio to the suburbs on the south bank of the Tejo. The busiest ferries are the *CP* company's ferry to the Barreiro railway station (runs from 5.45am to 2.45am) and the *Transtejo* company's ferry to Cacilhas, which services those wishing to see the grand Cristo Rei statue (runs between 6am

and 9.30pm. Note: the last ferry from Cacilhas to Praça do Comércio leaves at 9.10pm). Taking the ferry after dark is a beautiful way to see Lisbon by night. Tickets can be purchased on the platforms. For details call *CP* (Tel. 888 40 25) or *Transtejo* (Tel. 347 92 77).

## Organized Tours
To get a good idea of what Lisbon is about, you might like to join a guided tour. *Gray Line* (2-3 Av. Sidónio País, Tel. 53 88 46/ 57 75 23); *Cityrama* (12-13 Av. Praia da Vitória, Tel. 355 85 67/9; Praça Marquês de Pombal, Tel. 386 43 22); *Portugal Tours* (124 Rua D. Estefânia, Tel. 352 29 02/316 03 99) all offer daily three-hour tours covering most of the city's main sites.

During the summer, the *Carris* company offers a highly

recommended tour around the city in a special luxury tram. There are two routes to choose from: the city and its hills (*Linha das Colinas*) or the river route (*Linha do Tejo*). These multilingual tours leave several times a day from Praça do Comércio. Tel. 363 93 43 for further information.

Take one of *Transtejo*'s cruises up the Tejo to view Lisbon from the river. Available April through to October, these two-hour cruises leave from the marina at **Terreiro do Paço**. For further information, Tel. 87 50 58 or 86 41 00.

*Lisbon Walks* offers interesting walking tours in the Chiado, the Bairro Alto and the Baixa. The tours are led by professional guides, in a few languages. They are held between May-September, and last about three hours. The meeting point is Largo do Picadeiro, near São Carlos Theatre (Tel. 346 67 22).

**TOURING OUTSIDE THE CITY**

*Gray Line*, *Cityrama* and *Portugal Tours* offer a selection of guided tours to sites outside the city, such as Sintra, Mafra, Estoril and Cascais, Queluz, Nazaré and Óbidos.

*Sintra Tours*: the company specializes in jeep tours along the Sintra range to the Atlantic Ocean. You can go by the set route, or plan your own. (Tel. 923 41 45).

## Accommodation

Portugal has a wide selection of accommodation. The most expensive are the *pousadas*, historical sites that have been converted into government-owned hotels. Hotels are graded according to five categories; all have restaurants and room service.

Residentials (*residencial*) and pensions (*pensão*) are generally comfortable and well-kept. Residentials are larger than pensions and usually serve breakfast which is not always available at pensions. A night at a three- or four-star residential or pension will cost you the same as a one-star hotel, and is definitely a better bet.

Staying in a *quarto*, a room in

a private house (something like a bed-and-breakfast), is an inexpensive way to spend the night. Details are available from tourist information bureaus in the city.

Youth hostels are also inexpensive. Contact the *Associação Portuguesa de Pousadas de Juventude*, 46, Rua Andrada Corvo, 1000, Lisboa. Tel. 52 20 02 or 57 10 14.

## Hotels

### FIVE STARS
*Alfa Lisboa*: Avenida Columbano Bordalo Pinheiro, Tel. 726 21 21, Fax 726 30 31. Commercial area, ten minutes from airport.

*Altis*: 11, Rua Castilho, Tel. 52 24 96, Fax 54 86 96.

Central Lisbon, close to Parque Eduardo VII, shopping centre, entertainment spots. Good view of city.

*Avenida Palace*: 123, Rua 1 de Dezembro, Tel. 346 01 51, Fax 32 28 84. Between Rossio and the Praça dos Restauradores.

*Meridian Lisboa*: 149, Rua Castilho, Tel. 69 09 00, Fax 69 32 31. Overlooking Parque Eduardo VII.

*Ritz Inter-Continental*: 88, Rua Rodrigo da Fonseca, Tel. 69 20 20, Fax 69 17 83. Overlooking Parque Eduardo VII, luxurious and quiet.

*Hotel Tivoli*: Avenida da Liberdade, Tel. 53 01 81, Fax 57 94 61. Central. Over fifty years old.

### FOUR STARS
*Diplomático*: 74, Rua Castilho, Tel. 38 20 41, Fax 52 21 55. Near Parque Eduardo VII.

*Fénix*: 8, Praça Marquês de Pombal, Tel. 53 51 21, Fax 53 61 31. Modern.

*Flórida*: 32, Rua Duque de Palmela, Tel. 57 61 45, Fax 54 38 84. Close to Praça Marquês de Pombal in central Lisbon.

*Lisboa Penta*: Avenida dos Combatentes, Tel. 726 40 54, Fax 726 42 81. Pretty area. Five minutes from city centre.

*Lisboa Plaza*: 7, Avenida

Liberdade/Travessa do Salitre, Tel. 346 39 22, Fax 347 16 30. Very central. Beautiful decor.

*Novotel Lisboa*: 1642, Avenida José Malhoa, Tel. 726 60 22, Fax 726 64 96.

*Hotel Príncipe Real*: 53, Rua da Alegria, Tel. 346 01 16, Fax 342 21 04. Near Bairro Alto. Quiet.

*Zurique*: 18, Rua Ivone Silva, Tel. 793 71 11, Fax 793 72 90.

### THREE STARS
*Amazónia*: 12, Travessa da Fábrica dos Pentes, Tel. 387 70 06, Fax 387 90 90. Between Praça Marquês de Pombal and the Amoreiras shopping complex. Good view of the city. Plentiful parking.

*Capitol*: 24, Rua Eça de Quier, Tel. 353 68 11, Fax 352 61 65. Near Praça Marquês de Pombal.

*Eduardo VII*: 5-C, Avenida Fontes Pereira de Melo, Tel. 353 01 41, Fax 53 38 79.

*Jorge V*: 3, Rua Mouzinho da Silveira, Tel. 356 25 25, Fax 315 03 19. Between Rossio and Praça Marquês de Pombal.

*Rex*: 169, Rua Castilho, Tel. 388 21 61, Fax 388 75 81. Near Parque Eduardo VII. Pleasant.

*Hotel da Torre*: 8, Rua dos Jerónimos, Tel. 363 62 62, Fax 364 59 95. Near the beach and the Monastery of Jerónimos. Small, with good view of the city.

### TWO STARS
*Borges*: 108, Rua Garrett, Tel. 346 19 51, Fax 342 66 17. In the vicinity of the Chiado.

*Vip*: 25, Rua Fernão Lopes, Tel. 352 19 23, Fax 315 87 73.

*Metrópole*: 30, Praça Dom Pedro IV, Tel. 346 91 64, On Rossio Square.

*Suíço Atlântico*: Rua da Glória, Tel. 346 17 13. Central.

## Residentials and Pensions (*Pensões e Residenciais*)

### FOUR STARS
*Albergaria da Senhora do Monte*: 39, Calçada do Monte, Tel. 886 60 02, Not far from Alfama. Good view of the city.

*Residência Imperador*: 55, Avenida 5 de Outubro, Tel. 352 48 84, Fax 352 65 37. East of the Gulbenkian Museum.

*Residencial Nazareth*: 25-4, Avenida António Augusto de Aguiar, Tel. 54 20 16.

*Residência Roma*: 22-A1, Travessa da Glória, Tel. 346 05 57. Clean and comfortable.

*York House*: 32, Rua das Janelas Verdes; Tel. 396 24 35, Fax 397 27 93. Near the Museum of Ancient Art.

### THREE STARS
*Avenida Alameda*: 4, Avenida Sidónio País, Tel. 353 21 86, Fax 352 67 03. Next to Parque Eduardo VII.

*Residência Alicante*: 20-3/4, Avenida Duque de Loulé, Tel. 353 05 14; Fax 352 02 50. Near Praça Marquês de Pombal.

*Residência Horizonte*: 42, Avenida António Augusto de Aguiar, Tel. 353 95 26. Near Parque Eduardo VII.

*Pensão Portuense*: 153-1, Rua das Portas de Santo Antão, Tel. 346 41 97. Expensive.

*Residência Caravela*: 38, Rua Ferreira Lapa, Tel. 53 90 11, not far from Praça Marquês de Pombal.

*Residência Lisbonense*: 1, Rua Pinheiro Chagas, Tel. 54 46 28, Near Parque Eduardo VII.

*Residencial Luena*: 9, Rua Pascoal de Melo, Tel. 355 82 46, Fax 355 69 04. Not central.

### TWO STARS
*Pensão Londres*: 53-2, Rua Dom Pedro V, Tel. 346 22 03, In Bairro Alto.

*Pensão Estrêla do Chiado*: 29-4, Rua Garrett, Tel. 342 61 10, In the Chiado.

*Pensão Florescente*: 99, Rua das Portas de Santo Antão, Tel. 342 66 09, near the Praça dos Restauradores. Pleasant, clean, inexpensive.

*Pensão Flor dos Cavaleiros*: 58, Rua dos Cavaleiros, tel. 87 22 86, near Praça dos Restauradores.

*Pensão Beira Minho*: 2-6, Praça da Figueira, Tel. 346 18 46, in Baixa.

*Pensão Santiago*: 222-3, Rua dos Douradores, Tel. 888 43 53 in Baixa. Recommended.

*Pensão São João da Praça*: 92-7, Rua João da Praça, Tel. 888 13 78; Near Alfama.

#### CAMPING

*Parque Campismo de Monsanto*: In Parque de Florestal Monsanto; Tel. 760 89 38. Swimming pool, sport facilities and shopping.

## General Information

### Language

Portuguese is a blend of local dialects and Latin, which was brought to the region by the soldiers of the Roman Legion. Words and phrases from Arabic also found their way into Portuguese during the Moslem Conquest (711-1147). Portuguese is believed to have been established as a language

around 1300, when Dom Dinis came into power.

Despite clear similarities between Portuguese and Spanish, the latter will suffice only for basic communication in Portugal. Very few Lisboetans speak either English or French, but it shouldn't be difficult to get them to tell you prices, directions, etc. in one of these languages. In the tourist areas you will find many who speak foreign languages. It might be harder to get around without some knowledge of Portuguese in the residential areas and suburbs.

Voyages of exploration and imperialism transported Portuguese to all corners of the globe – from Brazil to Mozambique, from Goa to Cape Verde. The seventh most spoken language in the world

today, Portuguese is spoken by almost 180 million people.

The Portuguese generally take kindly to any attempt to speak their language. To study Portuguese while in Lisbon, contact the highly-recommended *Cial Language School* at 14, Avenida da República.

A brief dictionary at the end of the guide will help you with some essential phrases, and provide you with some ground rules for correct pronunciation.

## Tourist Services

When planning your trip to Portugal, there are several valuable sources of information. In most major cities in Europe, and in several major cities in North America, there are branches of the Portuguese National Tourist Office:

U.S.A.: 590, Fifth Avenue, 4th floor. New York, N.Y. 10036-4704. Tel. (212)354-4403/4, Fax (212)764-6137.

Canada: 60, Bloor Street West, Suite 1005, Toronto, Ontario M4W 3B8. Tel. (416)921 73 76, Fax 921 13 53; 500, Shurbrooke W Suite 930, Montreal – P.Q H3A 3C6. Tel. (514)843-4623, Fax 843-9328.

England: 22/25A Sackville Street, London W1X 1DE. Tel. (071) 494-1441, Fax 494-1868. Ireland: C/O Portuguese Embassy, Knocksinna House, Knocksinna, Fox Rock, Dublin 18. Tel. (031)289-3569, Fax (031)289-6852.

The *Municipal Tourist Information Bureau*'s main branch is in the ancient **Palácio Foz**, on Praça dos Restauradores. The bureau is open during the week from 9am-8pm; on Sun. between 10am-6pm (Tel. 346 36 24).

The *City of Lisbon's Tourism Department* is in **Pavilhão Carlos Lopes** in the Parque Eduardo VII (Tel. 315 17 36 or 315 19 15). There are other information bureaus at the airport, the passenger lounge, and on the first floor of the **Complexo das Amoreiras** shopping centre (Tel. 65 74 86).

You can get maps and guides from the news-stands on Rossio.

### CAR RENTAL
Car rental is relatively cheap in Portugal. You can rent a car on a daily or weekly basis from any one of several car rental companies (list below). To be

on the safe side, make sure the car rental company has a branch in the town you are heading for. Most companies will let you leave the car at your destination for no extra charge. You must be over 21, have a valid international driver's license and a credit card. You are advised to take out maximum insurance on the car.

Here are some of the car rental companies in Lisbon:

*Avis*: 14, Rua da Glória, Tel. 346 11 71, Fax 347 27 42.

*Budget*: 6, Avenida Fontes Pereira de Melo, Tel. 53 77 17, Fax 80 39 81.

*Europcar*: 24, Avenida António Augusto de Aguiar, Tel. 942 23 06, Fax 942 52 39.

*Eurodollar*: 124, Avenida António Augusto de Aguiar, Tel. 54 21 33, Fax 53 32 78.

*Rapauto*: 99, Rua da Beneficência, Tel. 793 32 58, Fax 793 17 68.

*Hertz*: 10, Avenida 5 de Outubro, Tel. 57 90 77, Fax 941 60 68.

*AA Castanheira*: 85A-89A, Avenida João Crisóstomo, Tel. 57 00 60, Fax 355 69 20.

**BICYCLE RENTAL**
*Eurolift*: 1-A, Escadinhas Marquês Ponte Lima, Tel. 888 50 02.

*Velo*: Casa da Ancôra (Tomadia), Praia das Maças, Sintra, Tel. 928 20 92.

## Currency and Exchange

The Portuguese *escudo* has been fairly stable over the past years, its rate changing only slightly in relation to the dollar or European currencies. The familiar dollar sign ($), placed before the cents (and not the dollars) is used to denote escudo in Portugal (ie., 500$00 is five-hundred escudos). There are coins of 1, 2$50, 5, 10, 20, 50, 100 and 200 escudos. Bills come in denominations of 500, 1,000, 2,000, 5,000 and 10,000. Each escudo is worth 100 (nigh-worthless) *centavos*.

You can change currency

(*câmbio*) at any local bank. The rate is the same at all banks, although the commission may differ – check before changing your money. Changing currency at the hotel will get you a lower rate than the banks. There shouldn't be any problem in changing most European currencies. You'll need a passport or ID document to change US$100 bills or travellers' cheques. Several automatic câmbios are positioned on Rossio. Check their rate and commission first.

All major credit cards (*cartão de crédito*) are accepted at leading tourist establishments in the city. Outside of Lisbon, credit cards are much less popular.

## Working Hours

**Banks** are open Mon. to Fri. 8.30am-3pm, although some branches break for lunch between 11.45am and 1pm. The branch on the Praça dos Restauradores is open from 9am-9pm. The bureau de change at the airport is open seven days a week until 11pm.

Many offices close for lunch between 1-2pm. **Government offices** are open to the public between 9am and 4.30pm.

Smaller **shops** are open Mon. to Fri., 9am-1pm and 3-7pm. Shops are open on Saturday mornings, and are closed on Sundays and holidays. Supermarkets and the new shopping centres are open from 9am to 11pm throughout the week. Local markets start up early in the morning; by 1pm the stalls generally close and the market-place is ready to be washed down. There are several colorful markets just outside Lisbon. A popular one is the **Feira de São Pedro** in Sintra.

**Post offices** are open Mon. to Fri., 9am-7pm. The post office on Praça dos Restauradores (opposite the Tourist Bureau) is open from 8am to midnight.

## Keeping in Touch

### TELEPHONES

Telephone lines out of Lisbon are not on par with the general standard in Europe, although there have been some major changes over the past few years. New switchboard systems have been installed; still, the phone system leaves much to be desired. Many telephone numbers have also been changed since the improvements.

To dial directly out of Lisbon: dial 00 for Europe and 097 for the rest of the world. To call collect, you can reach the operator at 099 (for Europe) and 098 (intercontinental). There's also a **central telephone office** near the National Theatre, on the northeast corner of Rossio, where you can call from one of the many telephones and pay on the spot.

Portugal's international code is 351; Lisbon's code is 1 (inside portugal – 01).

### POST

Lisbon's postal service (*correios*) is very efficient. You can get stamps (*selhos*) from post offices and tobacco stores with a **Selhos** sign outside. Portugal has beautiful stamps,

as do its former colonies, now independent, whose stamps are still available in Lisbon. For a small fee, you can have your mail sent to the main post office on Praça dos Restauradores. You'll need identification to get the letter.

Write to: Poste Restante, 58, Praça dos Restauradores, 1200 Lisboa, Portugal.

For further information about express mail (*Serviços de Correio Alelerado – DHL*) Tel. 814 31 90.

You can send **telegrammes** (*telegrammas*) from the post office or by phone – dial 183 (*CTT*) or 182 (*Marconi*).

**Newspapers** – English, French and German newspapers are easily found at the news-stands on Rossio, at the Santa Apolónia train station, and at the larger hotels and tourist

spots. Newspapers arrive within 24 hours and can cost double their regular news-stand price.

## Tipping

Waiters and taxi drivers are tipped 10%. Tip the bellboy about 150 escudos per suitcase, and the elevator-assistant, doorman, etc – about 100 escudos. If you have a personal tour guide, tip him or her about 1,500 for a half-day. Although your bill will usually include service, it is not uncommon to tip extra if you're pleased with the food and service.

## Time; Electricity

Lisbon is on GMT. Daylight savings time begins on the first Sunday of April, and clocks are turned back an hour on the first Sunday of October.

The electrical current in Portugal is 220 volts.

LISBON

# WHY LISBON?

As Portugal's capital for the past 700 years, Lisbon is a treasure chest of ancient art and artifacts filling the city's olden castles, churches and monasteries. If you're visiting Lisbon for the first time, a fascinating stay awaits you. This is the last city of the old world, and the first one of the new.

Modesty and moderation are the key words here. Lisbon doesn't offer the largest church, museum or diamond in the world; it is the most modest city in Europe. Palaces and churches, which else-where would have been converted into museums, continue to serve the community, just as the out-dated but beautiful trams and lifts are still an important means of transport for the city's inhabitants.

To get around the city you can take the Metro, trams or buses. Seeing the city on foot is still the best way to get to know it. You're likely to miss out on some unique and scenic spots if you take it all in from behind the wheel. The best way to absorb the atmosphere is to spend a few leisurely hours sitting at the sidewalk cafés on Praça Rossio or the Chiado; forget your worries, sit back for a while, and enjoy one of Lisbon's famous sweet pastries.

Like most interesting places, Lisbon has its other side. Join the excited crowds in the stands for a day at the bullfight, or the night-birds flocking to the narrow sidestreets of Bairro Alto for all-night

fun. Ancient streetlamps dimly light the *fado* singers roaming from one fado house to the next, and smell of cod and port wine fills the air.

Twice a week the **Thieves' Market** (Feira da Ladra) takes place at Campo de Santa Clara. It's best to come early to enjoy the mixture of friendly "types" offering their wares to the crowds of visitors. The Portuguese are an hospitable people, and a day at the Feira da Ladra is proof of it.

Some time before Portugal joined the EEC, the country

embarked on improving its roads, and travel is easier now than ever. A trip into the surrounding countryside to meet the villagers, or even a trip to the sea, can be just as pleasurable as time spent in the capital.

## LISBON

1. Praça Rossio
2. Teatro Nacional de Dona Maria II
3. Elevador de Santa Justa
4. Praça do Comércio
5. Rossio Station
6. Praça dos Restauradores
7. São Roque Museum of Sacred Art
8. Chiado
9. Carmo Monastery
10. Sé Patriarcal
11. Miradouro de Santa Luzia
12. Castelo de São Jorge
13. Mosteiro de São Vicente de Fora
14. Igreja de Santa Engrácia
15. Military Museum
16. Jardim Botanico
17. Praça Marquês de Pombal
18. Parque Eduardo VII
19. Calouste Gulbenkian Foundation
20. Amoreiras Shopping Complex
21. The Church of Madre de Deus
22. Tile Museum
23. Zoological Gardens
24. The Aqueduct
25. Basílica Estrêla
26. National Museum of Ancient Art
27. The 25th of April Bridge
28. Ajuda Palace
29. Campo Pequeno
30. Santa Apolónia Railway Station
31. Cais do Sodré Station

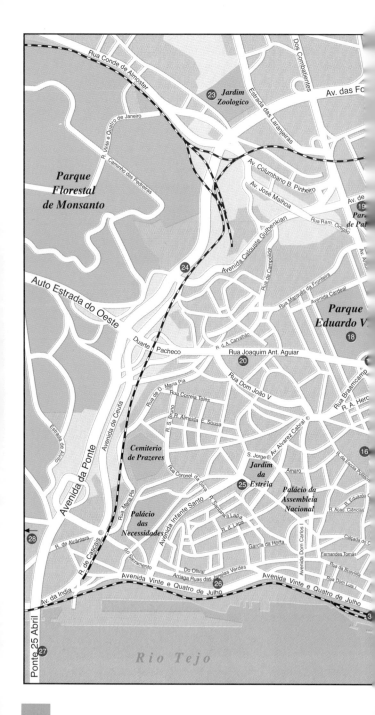

## The Baixa –
## The Heart of the City

Surrounded by hills, Baixa – the "low" quarter – has been the centre of commerce and government for over five centuries. A visit to Baixa will give you an idea of the character and pace of the city in general.

Baixa is a lively tourist area where the old and the new blend. Take a walk through the crowded squares, the impressive historical buildings and the sidewalk cafés. Begin the excursion at Praça Rossio, through Praça da Figueira and Praça do Comércio and end it at the beautiful staircase (Cais das Colunas) which descends to the Tejo River. The best way to get to Rossio, your starting point, is to take either the Metro to Rossio station, the tram (12, 28) or the bus (8, 14, 21, 31, 36, 37, 41, 43, 59).

*Rossio Square and Teatro Nacional de Dona Maria II*

On All Saints' Day (Todos-os-Santos) in 1755 most of Lisbon was gathered in the city's churches. At exactly 9:40am the earth began to tremble, and 15 minutes later the grand city centre was a pile of debris. Buildings tumbled to the ground and the tidal wave that followed flooded the royal palace and sank the ships in the harbor. The earthquake, fires and aftershocks killed tens of thousands and razed the entire commercial centre, as well as Portugal's houses of government and worship. The royal family, residing at Palácio de Belém in the western hills of the city at the time, was unharmed.

José I appointed his minister, José de Carvalho e Mello, better known as the Marquês de Pombal, to supervise the restoration of the city. Our tour through central Lisbon traces the Marquês de Pombal's vast project. To this day, the city centre is known as Baixa Pombalina.

Our point of departure in the heart of the city, **Praça Rossio**, is also known as Praça Dom Pedro IV. In the years preceding the earthquake, Rossio evolved from a small village into the centre of a powerful and independent city.

The large marble statue of Dom Pedro IV stands in the middle of the square. José Sales' statue of the 19th-century monarch depicts him with the Portuguese Constitution (*Carta Constitucional*) in his hand; at his feet are four women representing the virtues of a good ruler: justice, prudence, strength, and moderacy (a closer look at Dom Pedro's political record reveals he was not one to keep to the four basics).

**The Teatro Nacional de Dona Maria II** is on the northern part of the square. This is the site of the Palácio de Inquisição, where the *autos-da-fé* were conducted during the Inquisition. The palace, designed by Fortunato Lodi, did not survive the earthquake. Six pillars with Greek engravings stand in the front of the building. The figure of the father of Portuguese theatre, the 16th-century poet Gil Vicente, overlooks the square from its perch on the triangular roof. The 150 year-old Teatro Nacional has undergone restoration since a tragic fire damaged the place in 1964. It is worth going to see a play or musical, if only to get a glimpse of the building's magnificent decor, the President's royal box, the golden galleries and the red chairs.

*Teatro Nacional de Dona Maria II, in the northern part of Baixa*

On the west side of

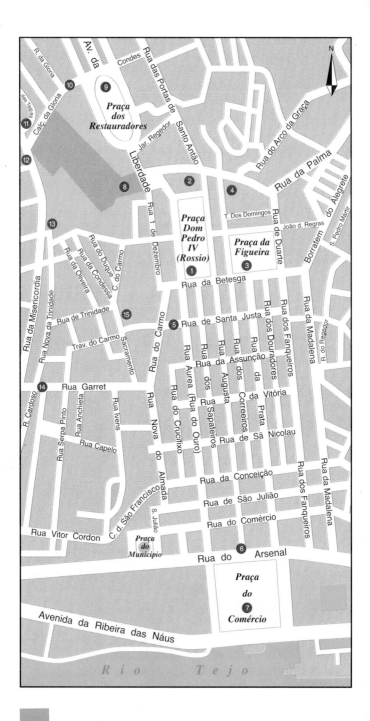

Rossio, among the modern cafés and electrical appliances stores, is the **Café Nicola**. Portugal's most famous café, it has been a home to the country's greatest artists since the 18th century and a meeting place for politicians, intellectuals and artists from the 19th century.

*Café Nicola has been a meeting place for politicians and artists for more than two centuries*

On the southern side of the square is the **Arco do Bandeira**, the archway leading onto the "Street of Shoemakers" (*Rua dos Sapateiros*). The archway, and the small flower market alongside it, are named after Domingo Bandeira, the owner of many buildings, one of the city's richest citizens. On the adjoining Rua do Bandeira, you can

### BAIXA AND BAIRRO ALTO

1. Praça Rossio
2. Teatro Nacional de Dona Maria II
3. Praça da Figueira
4. Igreja de São Domingos
5. Elevador de Santa Justa
6. Arco Monumental de Rua Augusta
7. Praça do Comércio
8. Rossio Station
9. Praça dos Restauradores
10. Elevador da Glória
11. The São Pedro de Alcântara look-out post
12. Palácio Ludovice
13. São Roque Museum of Sacred Art
14. Chiado
15. Carmo Monastery

*A view of the Baixa from the Castelo de São Jorge*

get superb cakes and pastries from the famous *Tendinha* bakery, established in 1840. At no. 227 you'll find another gem – one of the oldest cinemas in Europe, *Animatógrafo do Rossio,* where horror films and Ninja movies are shown regularly. This is just another example of the city's blending of old and new.

Back at Praça Rossio, the eastern side of the square borders on another small square, **Praça da Figueira**. A equestrian statue of Dom João I stands in the centre of the square. The 15th-century ruler was the founder of the Aviz Dynasty, the second dynasty of Portuguese kings. To the southeast, the Castelo de São Jorge overlooks the square. The Praça da Figueira was the city's main marketplace before the earthquake. The **Igreja de São Domingos**, situated between the Praça da Figueira and the Teatro Nacional, is recommended for those interested in churches and Christian art. Built on the ruins of an older 13th-century church, the Igreja de São Domingos was damaged by fire in 1959. Attempts at restoration have not come near reviving it to its former lost glory. Nevertheless, it is still worthwhile taking a look at this work of the 18th-century German-Portuguese architect, Ludovice (no entrance fee).

Returning to Rossio, go southwards to get an impression of the Marquês de Pombal's major reconstruction project. The Marquis "swept" the city centre clean of the piles of debris and built a neatly-planned area linking Praça Rossio to Praça do Comércio on the banks of the Tejo River. The main street, **Rua Augusta**, is the starting point for our southbound journey. On the streets running parallel to Rua Augusta tradesmen and craftsmen arranged themselves by profession; the "Street of Gold" (Rua do Ouro), the "Street of Silver (Rua da Prata), and the "Street of Shoemakers" are only a few examples.

Rua Augusta is closed off to traffic and generally crowded. The wine shop, *Macarios*, on 272, Rua Augusta was established in 1890, and sells excellent, though expensive, Portuguese wine.

Take a walk down any of the side streets leading off Rua Augusta. Large stores and smaller ones, flower-stands, cafés, street-performers and buskers add color to the tour. The **Elevador de Santa Justa** on Rua Santa Justa was built at the beginning of the 20th century by one of Eiffel's protégés. This unique lift is still in use today (see "Bairro Alto – The 'High Neighborhood'").

*Elevador de Santa Justa, connecting the "low" Baixa quarter with the Bairro Alto, the "high quarter"*

Rua Augusta joins up with Praça do Comércio, bordered by the **Arco Monumental de Rua Augusta**. Statues of the city's heroes adorn the top of this impressive archway: Virato, the Lusitanian rebel who fought the Romans; Nuno Álvares Pereira, who fought the Spaniards alongside João I in the 14th century; Vasco da Gama, who sailed to India; and the Marquês de Pombal. Flanking the city's heroes are mythological figures representing the Tejo and the Duoro Rivers. The gateway was built by the architects Costa and Santos as a victory arch commemorating Lisbon's recovery from the earthquake. A small arts and crafts fair is held daily at the foot of the archway.

Going through the archway, we enter Praça do Comércio, the historical centre of the city, also known as the "Palace Square" (Terreiro do Paço). Dom Manuel's 16th-century "Royal Palace on the River" (Paço da Ribeira) stood here for 250 years before the earthquake. The 70,000 books that filled the royal library were lost in the subsequent fire. The palace was never restored.

A 14-metre high statue of Dom José I, who ruled during the 1755 earthquake, was erected in the square. To build the 30-ton statue, the sculptor, Machado de Castro, used old canons from the royal armoury, and placed two carvings at the foot of the statue to symbolize victory and generosity. On the south side of the statue, an engraving depicts the work of the Marquês de Pombal. This reminder was removed after Dom José's death when the Marquês de Pombal was ousted from his high post. His image was restored 150 years later, by which time all the Marquês' adversaries had died.

*In the Baixa quarter*

After its restoration, parades and processions were held on the Praça do Comércio. This was also where Carlos I and his son were assassinated in 1908. In 1974, revolutionaries took over the square as one of the first sites of the uprising. The square was then transformed into a vast parking lot. The City of Lisbon has decided to restore the square and plans to turn it into a lively culture and tourist centre.

Cross over the square to the stairs, Cais das Colunas, leading down to the river. You can get a good view from here of the river and the ships docking in the port. Our tour ends here. You can either stroll back to the city centre, or continue on one of the other routes to the castle (see "Walls above the City –

From Praça do Comércio to Castelo São Jorge") or to the picturesque Alfama quarter (see "Alfama – A Journey into the Middle Ages").

*The Tejo – a view from Praça do Comércio*

## Bairro Alto – The "High Quarter"

The route takes us to the heart of Lisbon's historical entertainment area, Bairro Alto, the "high quarter." In past centuries, the quarter experienced quite reckless times, but it has changed over the past decades and is now quite safe to walk through during the day. Late at night, Bairro Alto changes its character. If you plan to spend a night out, you're advised to leave most of your money at the hotel.

Poor sailors and farmers seeking work at the port were the first to build their homes on these hills. Wine bars, brothels and small gambling establishments soon followed. The neighborhood on the hill expanded, attracting pleasure-seekers from all corners of the country.

A new type of music grew out of the neighborhood's heavy drinking, prostitution and gambling, a musical style that combined the poetry of the Middle Ages, Portuguese folk songs, and Moorish influences – *fado*, extremely popular in its homeland, is considered the folk music of Portugal.

*In Bairro Alto*

Our route begins at Praça Rossio, and goes through Praça dos Restauradores, Avenida da Liberdade, the São Roque Museum of Sacred Art (Museu de Arte Sacra de São

Roque). From there it continues to the Chiado, and finally to the famous elevator of Santa Justa (Elevador de Santa Justa) near Rossio.

Leaving from the northwest side of Rossio we arrive at **Rossio Station** (Estação do Rossio), dug into the hillside above Lisbon, and once the central train station of the city. All trains to and from the station travel through the tunnel. Two arches in the shape of horseshoes support the beautifully decorated window on the second and third floor of the building. Between the two Moorish-style arches is a statue of Dom Sebastião, who disappeared in battle in the 16th century and according to popular belief will reappear one day to save Portugal from her hardships. The splendid façade is the work of the architect José Luíz Monteiro and stands in contrast to the station's somewhat less impressive interior. Trains leave the Rossio train station for the city's northern suburbs and for Sintra. The information office is at the entrance to the station.

*Rossio station's decorated main entry, designed in alternating styles*

*The obelisk in Praça dos Restauradores, commemorating the 17th century liberation from Spain*

From the station go northwards to the **Praça dos Restauradoes** ("The Restorers Square") with its obelisk, commemorating Portugal's liberation from the 17th-century Spanish invasion. The bronze statues and marble carvings at the foot of the obelisk representing liberty and independence, are the work of the architect Fonseca (1886). Amongst the large shops and banks that fill the square is the Palácio Foz, housing the Ministry of Tourism's main information bureau.

Near the information bureau, and at

the beginning of Avenida da Liberdade, turn left on Calçada da Glória, which goes all the way up the hill. To get to the top, take the ornate **Elevador da Glória**, a funicular that has been taking passengers up to Bairro Alto for over a century.

At the top of the steep climb up Calçada da Glória, there's a **look-out post** in the São Pedro de Alcântara gardens, with a beautiful view of the Baixa below and of Castelo de São Jorge. A map (not up-to-date) made of colored tiles (*azulejos*) will help you to identify the sites.

Lisbon's largest collection of antique shops is on the Rua São Pedro de Alcântara and the adjacent Rua Dom Pedro V and Rua da Escola Politécnica. These small "museums" are worth a browse, even if you don't plan to buy anything. The engraved furniture, painted jars, ornamented mirrors and large clocks all add to the magical atmosphere.

Crossing over Rua São Pedro de Alcântara, opposite the gardens and observation post, stands the **Palácio Ludovice**, built in 1747 by the German architect, Ludwig. Ludwig, or Ludovice, as he later called himself, was brought by Dom João V to the royal court and planned most of the larger buildings of the time, the most impressive of which is the Mafra Monastery. Here you will also find a pub offering tastings of port wine.

*The famous Port of Portugal*

From Palácio Ludovice turn right onto Rua São Pedro de Alcântara until you get to a small square, **Largo Trindade Coelho**. Here stands the Igreja de São Roque, one of the city's most beautiful and important churches. Damaged in the 1755 earthquake, the Jesuit church's present façade is not as magnificent as it was, although its interior is quite awe-inspiring.

Construction of the Igreja de São Roque began towards the end of the 16th century on the foundations of a hermitage belonging to the Jesuit Order (then at the height of its power). Figures of the Jesuit leaders and founder, Ignacius de Loyola, can be seen within the church. The typical

*Lavish interior-decor in the Igreja de São Roque*

Jesuit architecture combining simplicty and force is evident in the high altar and in the chapels and sacred icons. The altar in the **Capela de São João Baptista** is a magnificent work of art. This gold and silver altar was made for Dom João V in Rome, and consecrated by the Pope himself several years before the earthquake.

The adjoining **Museum of Sacred Art of São Roque** (Museu de Arte Sacra de São Roque) houses an abundance of religious art from this and other Jesuit churches and monasteries. The church and the museum are open Tues.-Sun. 10am-1pm and 2-5pm, and closed on Mondays and holidays. During the week, Mass is held at noon, and on Sundays at 9am and 11am.

Going down Largo Trindade Coelho, you'll get to the grand restaurant at no. 20-C, Rua Nova da Trindade. *Cervejaria da Trindade* first opened in 1836, and has been serving

*The statue of the poet Fernando Pessoa in A Brasileira café*

Portuguese delicacies, and particularly fish and seafood ever since. Its three large halls are decorated with large paintings made from blue-white-and-gold tiles. There is also a small art gallery and an open-air terrace. Recommended (Tel. 342 35 06).

Turn right at the first

*The Gothic archways of Carmo Monastery survived the 1755 earthquake*

junction on Rua Nova da Trindade and left onto Rua de Misericórdia with its colorful and interesting little shops. The unique furniture store at no. 72, *Desigual*, has an interesting selection of African masks from Portugal's former colonies. Don't miss dinner at the elegant and renowned *Restaurante Tavares Rico* which opened in 1784 (!) on 35, Rua de Misericórdia.

Lisbon's fashionable shopping area, the **Chiado**, is at the end of Rua de Misericórdia. **Largo do Chiado**, a small and well-kept square adjacent to **Praça Luís de Camões**, is lined with beautiful mansions, bookshops, fashion houses and smart cafés. *A Brasileira*, the neighborhood's most famous café, and Lisbon's oldest, is at no. 120-122. A popular meeting place for writers in the 18th and 19th centuries, the café has statues of its patrons, the poets António Ribeiro and Fernando Pessoa.

Two streets away at the Teatro Nacional de São Carlos, ballet and opera lovers coming out of the Teatro São Luís mingle with actors and theatre-buffs after the show. Before deciding to settle in one of the neighborhood's cafés, take a walk around the Chiado to soak in its ambiance and beauty; they say the prettier and more "historical" the café, the blander its cakes and coffee!

Leaving the elegant square, turn left on the street near the *Borges Hotel* and right onto Rua da Trindade (don't get confused with Rua Nova da Trindade) where the **Carmo Monastery** (Convento do Carmo) is situated. Before the 1755 earthquake, this 14th-century monastery was the most magnificent in Lisbon. Its roof caved in during the earthquake, leaving only its

Gothic arches standing. The monastery, now an **Archeological Museum** (Museu Arqueológico), houses several relics from around the city. The building itself is more impressive than the exhibits (open Mon.-Sat. 10am-1pm and 2-5pm. Closed on Sunday. Entrance fee (call 346 04 73).

Our visit to Bairro Alto which began at the Elevador da Glória ends at another particularly beautiful elevator and a splendid panorama. A steel bridge to the right of the Carmo Monastery leads to **Elevador de Santa Justa**. Built in 1902 by Raoul Mesnier, the elevator was co-designed by Gustave Eiffel. The elevator is 30 metres high, and connects the "low" neighborhood, Baixa, to the "high," Bairro Alto. Tickets can be bought in the elevator. If you are planning an extended stay in the city, you'd better get the valuable public transportation guide (*Guia dos Transportes Públicos*) which is sold in the booth at the foot of the elevator. The elevator takes you back to the city centre, only a few streets away from Rossio.

*Elevador da Glória, the best way to go up the hill to Bairro Alto*

## Walls above the City – From Praça do Comércio to Castelo de São Jorge

Lisbon's hilltops all offer good opportunities for a panoramic view of the city, but the most spectacular of all is from the São Jorge Castle (Castelo de São Jorge). Although there is quite a difference in height between the city centre and the castle, the climb is not steep.

The route begins at **Praça do Comércio**; pauses at the Santo António Cathedral, and the Cathedral (Sé Patriarcal) of Lisbon, and then on to the castle overlooking the city (the castle can also be reached by taxi, bus 37 or tram 28). From the castle the route goes back down into the city centre. You can reach the starting point, Praça do Comércio, with most buses in the city, or by trams 15, 16, 18, 19, 24 and 26.

From Praça do Comércio turn east onto Rua Alfândega until you get to Rua da Madalena. Turn left here, and then right onto Rua de São Julião. Another left onto Rua da Padaria should get you to the **Largo da Sé,** the Cathedral's plaza.

The Cathedral's narrow piazza is sealed off on the left by Igreja de Santo António, which we will visit later, but first, back to **Sé Patriarcal**, on the southeast side of the square. You can't

*Lisbon's Cathedral – hints of baroque and Gothic influence*

miss the cathedral's splendid façade: its two square bell-towers and the large flower-shaped window above the round doorway (open all hours of the day, no entrance fee, except to go into the church's "treasure chamber").

Sé, the seat of Lisbon's bishopric, is an abbreviation of *Sedes Episcopales* (Episcopal Seat). As you enter you can get an idea of the church's thick fortress-like walls. The two bell-towers were also used as look-out posts in more precarious days. The church was originally constructed as a local shelter in times of danger.

The church has had a long and turbulent history. Originally the sacred centre of a Roman settlement, the small temple was probably transformed into a church when Christianity came to Portugal some 1,500 years ago. The Moors, who invaded the city in the 8th century, built a mosque on the ancient foundations which served them as a place of prayer for four centuries. In the 12th century, after Lisbon had been reconquered by Dom Afonso Henriques, the cathedral was rebuilt in the Romanesque style. Restoration work after various earthquakes has contributed Gothic and baroque elements to the church.

*Sé Patriarcal, the seat of Lisbon's bishopric*

The church's interior is free of ornaments and the walls are almost bare. On the left is the baptismal font decorated with ceramic tiles. Amongst those baptized here was Lisbon's adored saint, Santo António, born in the adjacent house. Behind the altar are several crypts with delicate carvings. Especially interesting is the one in which the fourteenth-century nobleman, Pacheco, and his wife are buried. His bearded figure with sword in hand is carved on his coffin. His faithful dog stands at his feet. His wife, holding a prayer book, also has a small dog at her feet. In the adjoining chapel are Dom Afonso and his wife Beatriz's coffins. The holy relics of Lisbon's patron saint, São Vicente, are kept in the church's sacred chamber (*Sacristia*).

*In Sé Patriarcal – the coffin of the 14th century nobleman, Pacheco*

São Vicente died in Spain during Emperor Diocletian's persecution

of early Christians in the fourth century. Crows, according to the legend, protected the saint's body from wild animals. Five hundred years later the body was found, in reasonable condition, and sent to the Algarve shores, safe from the heathen hand of the Moorish conquerors. When the ship carrying the saint's remains sank, his body was washed onto the shore of **Cabo de São Vicente**. Dom Afonso Henriques, founder of the Portuguese kingdom, ordered the relics brought to Lisbon, were they have been kept ever since. The chamber is closed to visitors for most of the year; on St. Vincent's Day, January 22, the relics are ceremoniously exhibited for the crowds of worshippers.

*The marble statue of São Vicente*

The entrance to the cloister (*claustro*) is to the left of the altar. This dusty and rather neglected area within the churchyard is crowded with Roman pillars, as well as Moorish and various remains from later periods.

Crossing over the square, we get to the modest **Igreja de Santo António**, built in honour of the saint known mainly for his humanistic preaching in Padua, Italy. Born in 1195, Santo António was baptized in the church we have just visited. He died in 1231. Outside of Portugal he is known as St. Anthony of Padua, the patron saint of the poor. Many miracles are attributed to Santo

### FROM BAIXA TO ALFAMA

1. *Praça do Comércio*
2. *Largo da Sé*
3. *Sé Patriarcal*
4. *Igreja de Santo António*
5. *Miradouro de Santa Luzia*
6. *Museu-Escola de Artes Decorativas*
7. *Castelo de Sáo Jorge*
8. *Church of the Conception*
9. *Casa dos Bicos*
10. *Fish Market*
11. *Igreja de São Miguel*
12. *Igreja de Santo Estêváo*
13. *Mosteiro de São Vicente de Fora*
14. *Igreja de Santa Engrácia*
15. *Military Museum*

*Miradouro de Santa Luzia offers a fine view of the Alfama quarter and the Tejo River*

António, particularly those having to do with good marriages. Young couples come to have their pictures taken on the steps of Igreja de Santo António, leaving behind bouquets of gratitude. Pictures and statues of the saint are on exhibit in the small gallery on the second floor. On St. Anthony's Day, June 13, a colorful all-night carnival circles the church (the gallery is open daily 10am-1pm and 2-6pm. Entrance fee).

Returning to the square, we walk up the hill on Rua Augusto Rosa and then onto Rua Limoeiro. We pass the Faculty of Law (Centro de Estudios Judiciários) on our way to Largo de Santa Luzia. From the square's scenic lookout post, **Miradouro de Santa Luzia**, you can get a fine view of the Alfama quarter, the harbor and the Tejo River. During the summer, a tourist information booth is open on the square.

From Largo de Santa Luzia we continue to the adjoining square, Largo das Portas do Sol. At no. 2 is the **Fundação Ricardo Espírito Santo**, also known as the **Museu-Escola de Artes Decorativas**, a research institute established to preserve Portugal's traditional crafts.

Ricardo Espírito Santo Silva, the member of an important family of bankers, was a devout amateur collector of local objets d'art. To preserve practical art and Portugal's regional crafts, he acquired a 17th-century castle, the **Palácio Azurara**, to house his collection. The palace, once part of the Castelo de São Jorge, overlooks the Alfama quarter and the Tejo River. Workshops are held in a wide range of practical centuries-old handicrafts. Students and researchers preserve the art of gold and silversmiths, as well as rug-stitching, embroidery, wood-carving, carpentry, bookbinding, and more. An exhibit of ancient pieces, alongside work by the institute's pupils, is on show at the museum (open Tues. and Thurs., 10am-8pm; Wed., Fri. and Sat., 10am-5pm. Closed on Mondays. Entrance fee. Call in advance if you wish to visit the workshops, Tel. 886 21 83).

From the north side of Largo das Portas do Sol we continue to another beautiful terrace, with a picturesque café beside the marble statue of São Vicente. Lisbon's patron saint holds a ship with the guardian crows in his hand. From the terrace you can look out on **Igreja de São Vicente de Fora** with its two towers, and the marble church of **Igreja de Santa Engrácia** resembling the Capitol building in Washington D.C. (see "Alfama – A Journey into the Middle Ages").

From Largo das Portas do Sol we climb the stairs at the edge of the square onto Rua Chão da Feira which leads to the impressive entrance to the **Castelo de São Jorge**, our final stop and definitely a highlight of a visit

*Igreja de Santo António*

to Lisbon. The castle is open daily from 10am until sunset; no entrance fee.

The Castelo de São Jorge has always been crucial to Lisbon's safety. From 110 metres above the city, the castle overlooks central Lisbon, the port and the Alfama quarter. First erected by the Romans, the Moors continued to fortify and renovate it. The Moslem fortress (Alcáçova) was conquered in 1147 by Portugal's first king, Afonso Henriques, and became the home of Portugal's monarchy for several generations. The **Paço Real de Alcáçova**, now a restaurant, has been witness to milestones in Portuguese history: this is where Vasco da Gama was welcomed home from his journey to India in the 16th century; the castle was seriously damaged in the 1755 earthquake, although large sections were subsequently renovated.

*The walls of Castelo de São Jorge – 110 metres above the city*

From the look-out towers, a great view of the city stretches out before us. The city's many lawns and parks, with their swans, ducks and peacocks, are all protected by law.

**Note**: As some of the paths leading onto the walls and up the towers are not completely safe, it is unadvisable to let children climb them unattended.

You can return to the city centre either the way you came or by tram 28. However the most pleasing and interesting way down is through the crowded neighborhood of workmen and fishermen. The small restaurants on the way down serve seafood at very cheap prices. Its worth wandering aimlessly through the maze of alleyways, taking in the sights, smells and flavours. At the bottom of the hill you'll find yourself in Baixa.

*A panoramic view from the walls of Castelo de São Jorge*

## Alfama — A Journey into the Middle Ages

A stay in Lisbon is incomplete without a visit to the **Alfama** quarter. Descendents of the quarter's first workers and fishermen still live in this thousand-year old labyrinth of narrow alleyways and beautiful old houses.

Since the beginning of the Bronze Age when semi-nomadic tribes first settled here, the Alfama quarter has been home to the city's invaders: the Phoenicians, the Greeks, the Carthaginians, and of course the Romans. Remains of a Roman amphitheater, built in 57 for Emperor Nero, still stand today on Rua São Mamede in the northern part of the quarter. (Termas dos Augustas, one of the Roman baths, can still be seen at the junction of Rua da Prata and Rua da Conceição, in Lisbon's Baixa.)

Once the Roman Empire had fallen in the 5th century, the quarter gradually began to decline. The Moorish invasion at the beginning of the 8th century brought the quarter back to life. Islam, then at the height of its prosperity, contributed new architectural concepts and advanced building methods to the city. Yet Lisbon never reached the astounding architectural achievements that made Toledo, Cordova, Seville and Granada grand cultural centres on the Iberian Peninsula. Nevertheless, Lisbon has many examples of the beauty Islam brought to the region. The Moors also built steam baths, or *al hamam*, the origin of the quarter's name, Alfama.

The Moors planned the structure of the quarter, surrounding it with a wall to protect the city. On October 24, 1147 Dom Afonso Henriques marched on the city (on the exact road where you are standing), and brought down the walls. New buildings were constructed, and the Christian monarchy took its residence at the **Castelo de São Jorge**. In the 15th and 16th centuries, the quarter's wealthier inhabitants began moving to other parts of the city. Dockhands and fisherman took their place, giving the quarter its present-day form and character. Over the years the quarter gradually deteriorated; a project to restore some 700 of its houses is presently underway.

Our tour of Alfama leaves from **Praça do Comércio**. Since the quarter's narrow streets make it difficult to enter by car, the best way to see Alfama is on foot. Although we will cover most of the architectural sites, roaming the quarter on foot is definitely the best way to feel the pulse of this part of Lisbon. During the day you needn't fear about getting lost; at night, on the other hand, it's less advisable to wander through the dark alleys alone.

From Praça do Comércio, turn down Rua da Alfândega, on the northeast side of the square. On the right hand side of the street is the beautiful **Church of the Conception** (Igreja da Conceição Velha). The Virgin Mary stands in the centre of its ornamented Manueline-style doorway, with Dom Manuel I himself, among others, kneeling before her. On what was once an old synagogue in Moorish times, Manuel I built a shelter for the poor (Misericórdia). Over the years, the shelter's chapel (Igreja da Misericórdia) expanded and the poor were moved elsewhere. Don't miss the impressive fresco on the church ceiling.

*Alfama is home to many who nestled on Lisbon's shores. In the background is the Pantheon of Santa Engrácia*

Several private bus service companies can be found further along Rua da Alfândega. You can get a bus from here to the Algarve coastline or to the north of the country. Buses leave from the large piazza, **Campo das Cebolas**. To the north of the

*The Feira da Ladra at Campo de Santa Clara is Lisbon's famous flea market*

piazza you can see the 16th-century **Casa dos Bicos**, its bricks made to protrude from the wall like diamonds. The house was built by the Braz de Albuquerque, then president of Lisbon's senate. Many members of the aristocratic Albuquerque family were involved in local politics. The 1755 earthquake destroyed two of the house's original four stories. The house has been closed to the public since 1983, when it was renovated by the city for an important European exhibition.

*Casa dos Bicos – House of the pointed stones*

Next, turn left off Cais de Santarém at **Arco de Jesus**, originally manned by the city's guards to protect it against potential naval attacks in the Middle Ages. At the top of the stairs, turn right onto Rua São João da Praça, into the heart of Alfama.

Rua São João da Praça joins up with Largo de São Rafael. The tower on this square is one of the only remains of the wall the Moors built around the city. Rua de São Pedro, on the east side of the square, is where the colorful and crowded **fish market** is held every day. The street continues eastward to **Largo do Chafariz de Dentro**, named after the city's first fountain, or *chafariz*, built by the Moors. To get to our next stop, the **Igreja de de São Miguel**, turn left onto Travessa São Miguel, which joins Beco do Pocinho and climbs up to Rua São Miguel. Turn left here to get to the church with the same name.

Like the quarter's other churches, Igreja de São Miguel stands out in its simplicty. Built in the 17th and 18th centuries, the church's wood ceiling carvings and decorated altar are particularly beautiful. From the Igreja de São Miguel you can climb the stairs to Rua Norberto Araújo to the **Santa Luzia lookout post** (Miradouro de Santa Luzia) (see "Walls above the City – From Praça do Comércio to Castelo de São Jorge").

*A residence in the Alfama quarter*

The small and inexpensive restaurants lining the surrounding squares are a good place to take a lunch-break. This is where the quarter's inhabitants go about their daily business. Watching the vendors at their stalls and the women doing laundry in the fountains, one can see how little things have changed over the years.

Back on your feet, take a left off Rua São Miguel for a glimpse at **Beco da Cardosa**, one of Alfama's most quaint and picturesque side-streets. Carry on up Rua São Miguel until it widens onto the small square, joining up with Rua da Regueira.

Look out for the small alley leading off Rua da Regueira, Beco de Carneiro ("Alley of Sheep"). The alley is so narrow and the

*The entrance to the Military Museum, with an imposing statue on top of the archway*

houses so tightly packed that the roofs seem to overlap. Beco de Carneiro leads to **Igreja de Santo Estêvão**. Originally built in the 13th century, this church has been repeatedly renovated, and is larger than other churches in the quarter.

From Igreja de Santo Estêvão, in the eastern part of the quarter, you can carry on northwards via Rua Braga to the beautiful Largo do Salvador and to the Castelo de São Jorge. You can alternately continue along Calçada de São Vicente to the church of the same name.

## Beyond Alfama

Although the quiet residential areas to the north and east of the Alfama quarter are not a tourist attraction, they do not lack places of interest. The three buildings that attract the most attention are the **Mosteiro de São Vicente de Fora** ("São Vicente Outside the Walls"), the monastery where Portugal's monarchs are buried; **Igreja de Santa Engrácia**, the church that took 284 years to build; and the **Military Museum** (Museu Militar) at the bottom of the hill near the river. If you have spare time on your hands, these sites are well worth a visit.

The **Mosteiro de São Vicente de Fora**'s history goes back to the 12th century, when the Crusaders joined up with Afonso Henriques to reconquer Lisbon from the Moors. The German forces stationed on this site promised Lisbon's patron saint, São Vicente, they would build a monastery for him if they won the battle. The battle was won, and in the mid-15th century, Afonso Henriques made good his promise. The original building was destroyed 400 years later and a new and impressive church was built in its place. The economic prosperity of the 16th and 17th centuries made a particularly grand monastery affordable. The touch of the Italian architect brought to Portugal to design the monastery, Terzi, is quite evident in the splendid façade and vast and ornamented entrance hall.

A wooden door off to the right of the entrance leads onto the monastery's cloisters (*claustro*). Colorful ceramic-tiles (*azulejos*) from the 18th century, depicting La Fontaine's fables, line the walls of the cloisters. Near the cloisters is the Pantheon of the Bragança monarchs, who ruled Portugal from the mid-17th century. (Entrance fee for the cloisters. Open daily, 10am-2pm).

Lisbon's centuries-old flea-market, the **Thieves' Market** (Feira da Ladra), is held every Tuesday and Saturday near the monastery on the Campo de Santa Clara (turn to the "Filling the Basket: Where to Shop for What" section for more information on the city's markets).

*Igreja de Santa Engracía, the church that took almost 300 years to build!*

*A view from the church
of Santa Engrácia*

Dominating the view beyond the flea-market is a rather large marble church, the **Igreja de Santa Engrácia**. A smaller church by the same name was erected on this site some 400 years ago by Dona Maria, the daughter of Manuel I. A royal favorite, the church was adorned with sacred art and silver. In 1630 the host was stolen from the church, and Simão Solis, a young Jewish merchant, was accused of desecrating the holy site. His hands were amputated and his body burnt at the stake. When it was later revealed that the youth had sought to protect the honour of a young nun he had met, the city's inhabitants raised money to build a grander church on the site. Construction began immediately and was completed some 280 years later! A common saying in Lisbon, "Obras de Santa Engrácia," has come to mean "a job never done."

The church, which is also the site of the **National Pantheon**, is built in the shape of a cross and has a magnificent interior. The view from the church tower (which can be reached by lift) is far more fascinating than the Pantheon's tombs. (Entrance fee).

The **Military Museum** is only a short walk from the Igreja de Santa Engrácia. In the

16th century, the building was a cannon foundry and, for centuries, an ammunition dump for the Portuguese army. The museum has an interesting collection of arms and ammunition from the days of the Christian conquest to the First World War.

Lisbon's military museum lies close to the river and to the Estação Santa Apolónia, the city's largest international railway station. To get to the museum, take any bus going to the station. (Open Tues.-Sun., 10am-4pm. Closed on Mondays and holidays. Entrance fee, except on Wednesdays. Tel. 888 21 31).

*The classic façade of the National Pantheon*

## The Greenfields of Lisbon – From Praça dos Restauradores to Parque Eduardo VII

Like the route through Baixa, this tour is a fine opportunity to become acquainted with modern Lisbon.

Our tour of the valley between the eastern and western hills begins at Praça dos Restauradores, near Rossio. We'll visit the Botanical Garden, Praça Marquês de Pombal, and end at the Calouste Gulbenkian Foundation.

You can reach the Praça dos Restauradores either by Metro (Restauradores Station) or by bus. North off Praça dos Restauradores is the Avenida da Liberdade, lined with evergreen palm trees. Named in honor of Portugal's liberation from Spanish rule, the Avenida da Liberdade is modern-day Lisbon's main thoroughfare. Along the boulevard, known simply as "A Avenida," are large hotels, shopping centres, banks, travel agencies, etc.

*Avenida da Liberdade, broad and elegant, lined with evergreen palm trees*

Stay on the right (east) side of the road, and turn right off Largo da Anunciada and

across Rua Portas de Santo Antão to the **Lavra Elevator** (Elevador do Lavra).

The Elevador do Lavra goes from the city centre in the valley to Rua Camara Pestana at the top of the hill. Built in 1884 by one of Gustave Eiffel's protégés, Mesnier, this was Lisbon's first elevator. From the **Miradouro do Torel** look-out post you can get a bird's-eye view of the entire route: from Praça dos Restauradores, via the boulevard, all the way to Parque Eduardo VII and the *Amoreiras* shopping complex.

The stairs back down to the boulevard will take you to Rua do Telhal, which joins up with Rua das Pretas. Cross over "A Avenida" to Praça da Alegria which leads you to Rua da Alegria and eventually to the **Jardim Botanico**.

Lisbon's Botanical Garden covers an area of 35,000 sq/m and was originally built towards the end of the 19th century as part of the **Faculty of Sciences** (Faculdade de Ciencias). The Faculty's large building on the northwestern corner of the garden has a

*Parque Eduardo VII, with the statue of Marquês de Pombal in its southern end.*

variety of scientific exhibitions. Still, it is
much more interesting to explore the paths
outside, with their trees, flowers and cacti
from all corners of the globe. (Open daily

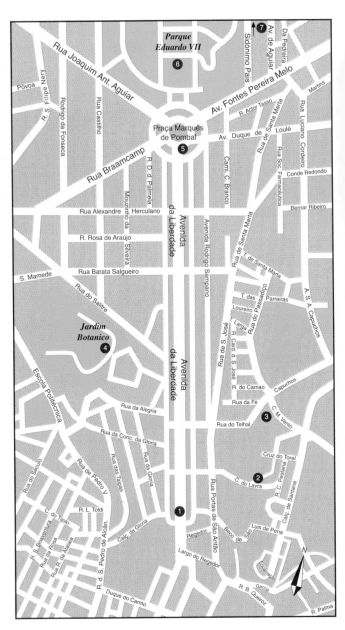

*In the Jardim Botanico – exhibitions from all over the world*

from 10am till just before sunset. Entrance fee).

Getting back to the boulevard, we continue northwards to the **Praça Marquês de Pombal**. At the centre of this round square, also known as "Rotunda," is the statue of the Marquês de Pombal, the man responsible for reconstructing Lisbon after the 1755 earthquake. The vigorous ex-minister set out to rebuild the city under the slogan: "Bury the dead and look after the living" ("Sepultar os Mortos, Cuidar dos Vivos"). The unpopular but ambitious marquês was pushed out of public office in 1777 after the death of his patron, Dom José I. Dona Maria I ordered Pombal's image removed from various sites around the city, including the one at the base of Dom José's equestrian statue in Praça do Comércio. With the revival of liberal values in the mid-19th century, the marquês was given the respect due to him: The lion on his

---

*FROM PRAÇA DOS RESTAURADORES*
*TO PARQUE EDUARDO VII*

*The impressive statue of Marquês de Pombal, the restorer of Lisbon after the 1755 earthquake*

*In the Calouste Gulbenkian statue park*

statue symbolizes his powerful and important role in the capital's history.

The Praça Marquês de Pombal is also the gateway to the city's main park, **Parque Eduardo VII,** with its geometrically pruned box hedges and large sports centre. Originally Parque da Liberdade, the park was renamed to commemorate Edward VII's visit to Portugal in 1902. The **Pavilhão dos Esportes** on the eastern side of the park is named after Portugal's Olympic marathon runner, Carlos Lopes. Alongside the pavillion with its magnificent 300 year-old tile scenes, is a pleasant café and a small pond. The two pillars at the top of the park commemorate Queen Elizabeth II's 1957 visit to Lisbon.

On the western side is the park's most beautiful attraction, the **Estufa Fria**. This 200-metre long glass house has a variety of plants and "landscapes." Enjoy a slow walk among the waterfalls and rare tropical plants, and visit the new adjoining section built especially for non-tropical plants. The Estufa Fria is open all day and is highly recommended. At night, on the other hand, the park can be dangerous. (Entrance fee).

A large **book fair** (Feira da Livro) is held in the park every May.

### BEYOND THE PARK

A very interesting place to visit within walking distance from the Parque Eduardo VII is the **Calouste Gulbenkian Foundation** (Fundação Calouste Gulbenkian), which attracts large crowds of visitors. It can be reached on foot going northwards along Avenida António Augusto de Aguiar, or by bus

(31, 41, 46) or Metro (São Sebastião Station). This centre of Modern Art is on 45 Avenida de Berna and is open Tues.-Sun., 10am-5pm; closed Mondays and holidays. Entrance fee. Tel. 795 02 36.

This cultural complex includes a museum which houses Gulbenkian's outstanding private collection, the Centre of Modern Art, a statue park, modern auditoriums, a theatre, an amphitheatre and conference rooms – all aimed at encouraging and supporting Portuguese culture. Constructed over the past three decades, these buildings are wonderful examples of late twentieth-century architecture.

*Estufa Fria, a 200-meter long glass house with rare tropical plants*

Gulbenkian, the late Armenian multi-millionare, was born in Turkey in 1869 to a respected family of merchants. During his studies in London, Gulbenkian became involved in the oil business and established the *Iraq Petroleum Company* over a century ago. Because he made five percent from all the company's major deals, Gulbenkian earned himself the nickname "Mr. 5%." During the First World War, the oil magnate moved to neutral Portugal, where he lived until his death in 1955.

*The Calouste Gulbenlian Museum houses a rich collection of traditional as well as modern art*

*Calouste Gulbenkian*

An almost compulsive art-lover, he was lucky enough to have the means to indulge his "hobby" and put together one of the finest private collections in the world. As a token of gratitude to his new home, Gulbenkian set up a foundation to encourage local art. This foundation supports numerous cultural, projects including the philharmonic orchestra, a choir, a ballet company, museums and a library with 130,000 books devoted mainly to Portuguese art.

The **Calouste Gulbekian Museum's** fine collection reflects the many aspects of Gulbenkian's character. The section devoted to Middle-Eastern and Islamic Art contains Egyptian art from the third century BC, an Assyrian bas-relief from the ninth century BC, and 14th-century mosque lamps from Syria. The Armenian manuscripts from the 12th to the 14th centuries are particularly fascinating, as are the rugs and carpets from different periods. The Greek and Roman exhibition has a large collection of gold and silver coins. There are also exhibits of Chinese and Japanese porcelain and prints from the 13th to the 19th century. The wonderful view from the museum's windows is no less beautiful than the exhibitions within.

In the collection of European art are 14th-century ivory statues, Flemmish and Italian wall-hangings from the 16th century, and works by Rembrandt, Rubens, Van Dyck and Turner, to name but a few. The impressionists are well-represented by Manet, Monet,

Renoir and Degas. An entire section is devoted to the 18th-century Venetian artist, Francisco Gaudí, and another to the eccentric work of the French artist, René Lalique, a personal friend of Gulbenkian's.

*The Calouste
Gulbenkian Museum*

## Belém – The Jewel of the Sea

Conveniently situated on the western point of the continent and on the shores of the Atlantic, Portugal was a leading maritime power for centuries. The country's fleets brought home great riches from the colonies in Africa, Asia, and Brazil. Portugal's able mariners ruled many of the main trade routes.

Belém is a priceless architectural gem, and shouldn't be missed on any visit to Lisbon. Belém's history goes back to the 13th and 14th centuries when it was just a small fishing village outside of Lisbon. During the 15th century when Portugal's colonial concerns flourished, Belém, being at the mouth of the Tejo River, became a bustling port of departure for the great sea expeditions. As Lisbon developed and expanded, Belém was incorporated into the city; far from the maddening urban crowd, it became a favorite seat for royalty and the aristocracy. (When the earthquake hit the city centre in 1755, the royal family were fortunately residing at the palace in Belém).

Today, Belém has numerous museums and maritime monuments, but above all – the **Monastery of Jerónimos** (Mosteiro dos Jerónimos), probably Lisbon's most splendid and fascinating building. A visit to Belém will take up the better part of the day, and is without

*Boats in the Belém docks, once serving as the departure point for maritime adventure*

a doubt one of the highlights of a stay in Lisbon. The route begins at the **National Coach Museum** next to the bus and tram station, proceeds to the Monastery and its museums, continues on to the **Monument to the Discoveries** (Padrão dos Descobrimentos), and ends at the **Tower of Belém** (Torre de Belém), a beacon for home-coming sailors.

Belém lies six kilometres to the west of the city centre and can be reached by bus (27, 28, 43 from Praça do Comércio), by train (*comboio*) from Cais do Sodré, or by tram. The best way to get there is by trams 15, 16 or 17 – all of which go through Praça do Comércio. Your ride to Belém takes you past the large

*Royal carriages on display in the National Coach Museum*

bridge over the Tejo and through the crowded and colorful streets. Look out for the Communist Party's large murals on Avenida da 24 de Julho depicting the workers overthrowing the former regime.

## THE NATIONAL COACH MUSEUM (MUSEU NACIONAL DOS COCHES)

What might sound like an uninteresting site, and reason enough to head straight for the Monastery of Jerónimos, is actually one of the finest and most extraordinary coach museums in the world. A variety of exquisite coaches are on exhibit in halls no less splendid, adding to the regal aura of the entire museum. (Open Tues.-Sun. 10am-1pm and 2.30-5pm; closed on Mondays and holidays. For students, disabled and OAPs no entrance fee. Sunday mornings free. Tel. 363 80 22).

The National Coach Museum is on **Praça Afonso de Albuquerque** in one of the wings of the ancient Palácio de Belém, the official home of Portugal's President. From the entrance to the museum you can see the ceremoniously-clad guards outside the Presidential palace. Large crowds gather to watch the changing of the guard every few months.

The Nobility Lounge (Salão Nobre) with its 17th and 18th-century coaches, and the horse-riding arena (Picadeiro Real) are the museum's main sections. The arena, which once served the Royal Riding School, was a special wing bought by Dom João V from a local nobleman. Built towards the end of the

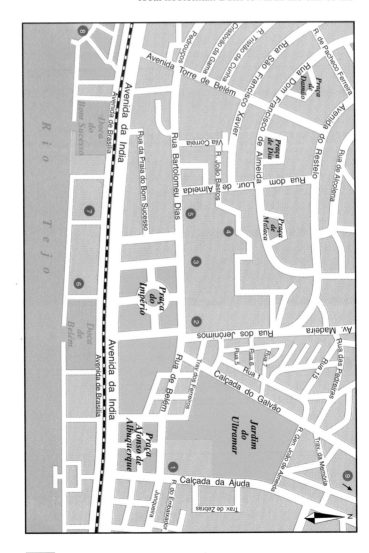

18th century, the arena was designed in the neo-classical style by the Italian architect, Giacomo Azzolini. The royal family would watch from the top floor. In 1911, a year after Portugal became a republic, the royal arena became the coach museum.

*Mosteiro dos Jerónimos. Manuel I built this grand monastery on the spot of Vasco da Gama's embarkment*

A survey of the impressive coaches – from King Felipe II of Spain's 16th-century coach to the 19th-century ornate and elegant "coronation coach" – is a lesson in technological development and design in the days before mechanical transportation. The carriages differ in materials, style and luxury.

### THE MONASTERY OF JERÓNIMOS (MOSTEIRO DOS JERÓNIMOS)

Adjacent to the National Coach Museum is one of Lisbon's most outstanding sites and a perfect example of Manueline architecture, the Monastery of Jerónimos. This is a must! (Open Tues.-Sun., 10am-5pm; closed Mondays and holidays. Entrance fee. Tel. 362 00 34).

### BELÉM

1. National Coach Museum
2. Monastery of Jerónimos
3. National Museum of Archeology and Ethnology
4. The Planetarium
5. Maritime Museum
6. Monument to the Discoveries
7. Museum of Popular Art
8. Tower of Belém
9. Ajuda Palace

A statue of Prince Henry the Navigator and scenes from the life of São Jerónimo adorn the southern entrance to the monastery. There is also a distinctive statue of Our Lady of Bethlehem (Nossa Senhora de Belém) over the entrance. The other entrance from the west is decorated with statues of Manuel I, who lay the foundations for the monastery, his wife Dona Maria, São Jerónimo, João the Baptist, and others, all sculpted by Nicolas de Chanterene. These two magnificent doorways are the work of the architect, Diogo de Boitaca.

Turn right through the main western door. The 30-metre high columns get gradually narrower, creating an optical illusion that makes the actual size of the interior look larger. The church's uncharacteristically large size shows the respect and admiration the Portuguese rulers had for the country's great explorers.

A young Portuguese navigator by the name of Vasco da Gama left Belém in 1497 on a voyage to India. Before embarking on his expedition, the 29-year old seafarer said his prayers at a small chapel in Belém. Dom Manuel I swore to build a grand monastery on the site if the voyage was a success. Five

*A map of the world at the foot of the Monument to the Discoveries*

years later, after da Gama discovered the route to India, Dom Manuel ordered the construction to begin. Work on the Monastery of Jerónimos continued throughout the 16th century. Vasco da Gama, who died in India in 1524, is buried in the church. His grand tomb is to the left of the western door; and to the right – the tomb of Portugal's national poet, Luís de Camões.

*Intricate stone carvings in the Monastery of Jerónimos*

Coffins of the Aviz royal house, rulers of Portugal until the Spanish conquest in 1580, are in the small chapels around the altar. The founder of this great church, Manuel I, is buried in the central chapel with his wife, Dona Maria, his son, Dom João III and his bride, Dona Catarina. The elephants carrying the coffins are reminders of a strange fight arranged by Dom Manuel in 1515 between an elephant and a rhinoceros to determine which was the stronger animal. It was a short fight. The rhinoceros huffed and puffed and the elephant fled the arena. The king sent the rhinoceros as a gift to the Pope by ship but it sank before reaching the Italian shores.

Turn right out of the western door to get to the monastery's magnificent tier and galleries (you'll need to buy a ticket before climbing the stairs). Built by two of the church's initial architects, Diogo de Boitaca and João de Castilho, the tier is considered to be one of the most splendid in Europe. Its two storeys are adorned with intricate stone carvings and exquisite fountains; all typical examples of the Manueline style.

The monastery's western wing houses the **National Museum of Archeology and Ethnology** (Museu Nacional de Arqueologia and Etnologia) with its rather conventional archeological and cultural exhibitions – from primitive tools to Roman statues. Open Tues.-Sun. 10am-12pm and 2-5pm; closed Mondays and holidays. Entrance fee. Students and children under 14 – free. Tel. 362 00 00. To the west of the monastery is the **Planetarium** (Planetário), built with funds from the Gulbenkian Foundation (see "The Greenfields of Lisbon – From Praça dos Restauradores to Parque Eduardo VII"). Opposite the Archeological Museum is another museum, the **Maritime Museum** (Museu da Marinha), where sea-lovers and children can enjoy an interesting collection of remodeled and restored sailing vessels, navigating equipment, old maps and even two airplanes. One of the planes, the *Santa Cruz*, crossed the South Atlantic Sea in 1927. (The Maritime Museum is open Tues.-Sun. 10am-5pm; closed Mondays and holidays. Entrance fee. Free for children under 10 and adults over 65; Children aged 10-18 half-price. Free on Wednesdays. Tel. 362 00 10).

## THE BELÉM DOCKS (DOCA DE BELÉM)

There was a time when the monastery stood on the water's edge. The past centuries have reshaped the shores of the Tejo River and the docks. To get to the modern **Monument to the Discoveries** (Padrão dos Descobrimentos) we must cross the Praça do Império and the public park with its comfortable benches and look-out post.

*The Monument to the Discoveries, built to commemorate 500 years to the death of Henry the Navigator*

Designed in the shape of a caravel, the Monument to the Discoveries was built in 1960 to commemorate 500 years since the death of Prince Henry the Navigator. On the ship's prow are images of Portugal's leading historical figures, amongst them Henry the Navigator, one of the progressive forces in the country's great maritime and colonial past.

Turning left along Avenida de Brasilia, there are somewhat less attractive tourist sites: restaurants, an **Aquarium** (Espelho da

*If wishing to enrich your knowledge about Portugal's nautical history – pay a visit to Lisbon's Maritime Museum*

*Doca de Belém – Lisbon's marina*

Água), the **Museum of Popular Art** (Museu de Arte Popular) with a colorful selection of traditional crafts.

On the southwestern end of Belém is the ornate **Tower of Belém** (Torre de Belém), another fine example of Manueline architecture, is a truly beautiful and exciting historical treasure. Manuel I built this fortress in the 16th century to protect the monastery and the port. The original construction, the **Castelo de São Vicente**, stood in the water, and for centuries was the image of home for Portugal's sailors. Between the years 1580 and 1828 the castle was used as a prison. Open Tues.-Sun. 10am-5pm; closed Mondays and holidays. Entrance fee. Tel. 301 98 06.

On your stroll back to the tram or bus station opposite the Coach Museum you can stop to taste the famous *Pasteis de Bélem* (Belém pastries) at any of the nearby restaurants and cafés.

### THE NATIONAL AJUDA PALACE (PALÁCIO NACIONAL DA AJUDA)

Not far from where our tour of Belém ends lies another interesting site.

A major turning point in Lisbon's history, the earthquake of 1755 caused many Lisboetans, particularly the royal family and the aristocracy, to move to the outskirts of the city. At the beginning of the 19th century, construction began here on a palace. Never fully completed, the Palácio da Ajuda is still the largest palace in Lisbon. It was designed by José da Costa and Francisco Fabri to resemble the royal palace in Naples, Italy.

Dom Luís I (1861-1889) made the palace his home as late as the 1860s. The royal family continued to live here until Portugal became a republic in 1910. The palace's rooms are filled with 19th-century furniture, paintings and statues collected over the years by the royal family.

The palace, now a national museum, can be reached by bus (14 from Praça da Figueira) or by tram (18 from Praça do Comércio). Open Thurs.- Tues. 10am-5pm; closed on Wednesdays and holidays. Entrance fee. Tel. 363 70 95.

*The National Coach Museum by night*

## More to See

### The Church of Madre de Deus and The Tile Museum (Museu dos Azulejos)

One of Lisbon's most important religious sites is about 2km northeast of the Santa Apolónia train station. Although some distance from the city centre, it is well worth a visit. The Church of Madre de Deus is one of the richest and most beautiful in the city. In the 1980s a Tile Museum was established in the adjacent monastery.

*The entrance to the church of Madre de Deus, a favorite with the ladies of the aristocracy*

You can get to the church by public transportation from Baixa (trams 3 and 16) and from Belém by bus 42. The museum is open Tues.-Sun. 2-5pm; closed Mondays and holidays. Entrance fee. Students, children under 14 and OAPs – free. Entrance to the church is free. Tel. 814 77 47.

The Manueline ornamental design in the entrance is virtually the only reminder of the church's 250 years of activity before the earthquake in 1755. The entire complex was erected in 1509 by Dona Leonor, Dom João II's widow. The monastery became a favorite place of prayer for the ladies of the aristocracy and the court, particularly those wishing to become pregnant.

The visitor immediately finds himself surrounded by ornate gilded decorations, wood carvings and pictures on the church walls and ceiling. These treasures were moved to the entrance after the earthquake, and remained there until the last of the nuns died in the mid-19th century.

In the western wing of the church, in what used to be the monastery, is the **Tile**

**Museum** (Museu dos Azulejos). You will need to buy a ticket for the museum.

Anyone walking through the streets, palaces and churches of Lisbon will be delighted by the many colorful *azulejo* murals and panels. The word *azulejos*, or ceramic tiles, is from the Arabic "*al Zulej*" meaning "small filed stones placed together." Because many of the ceramic tiles are blue and white, tourists often make the mistake in thinking the word is from the Portuguese for "blue" – *azul* (it, too, an Arabic word).

This art form probably goes back to Roman times when milestones were decorated with mosaics. In the 15th century, the tiles were originally purple, yellow and blue. Only in the 18th century, when Dutch (Delft) porcelain came to Portugal, did blue begin to dominate the colored tiles.

The museum's exhibit follows the evolution of the different colors and styles. Don't miss the picture of Lisbon before the fatal earthquake, on the second floor. Ancient Spanish and Portuguese tiles are exhibited throughout the museum, as well as modern attempts to keep this art alive. There is also a small workshop demonstrating how ceramic tiles are made.

### Zoological Gardens (Jardim Zoológico)

Lisbon's zoo is a favorite spot for children. It is, however, in serious need of repair, both for the good of the animals and of the visitors. Kids will enjoy the wide variety of animals and the various performing acts. This tranquil garden-like zoo hosts over half a million visitors a year. Children are given the opportunity to help feed the animals at 4pm feeding time.

To get to the zoo, take either the Metro (Laranjeiras station) or the bus (15 from Praça do Comércio, or 31, 41, 46 from Rossio). The zoo is open daily 9am-8pm. Entrance fee.

### The Aqueduct (Aqueduto das Águas Livres)

For centuries Lisbon had to deal with a shortage of drinking water for its growing population. Construction of an aqueduct, completed in 1748, ensured the city's inhabitants easy access to free water (*águas livres*). The aqueduct stretches for 18km from the Canecas springs into Lisbon. According to the original plan, the aqueduct was to reach Rossio in the city centre. However, due to financial and planning difficulties, the aqueduct only reaches the

*The Aqueduct*

*The Basílica da Estrêla, built, as vowed, by Dona Maria I with the birth of her child*

Amoreiras quarter, with its colorful modern shopping centre.

At the point where the aqueduct ends, an arch (Arco das Amoreiras) was built to celebrate the arrival of water to Lisbon in 1748. The aqueduct continued to serve the city until recently. Since you'll be able to follow the aqueduct on your drive through the city, you may not want to go out of your way to visit its exact endpoint. To get to the arch in the Campolide quarter, take a taxi, or tram 24 from Praça do Comércio, or else bus no. 2 from Rossio.

## Basílica da Estrêla

The church's spectacular beauty and its lush gardens have made it a popular site. Towards the end of the 18th century Dona Maria I vowed that if she and her uncle, Dom Pedro II, were blessed with son, she would build a grand church; ten months later construction began. The church's beautifully proportioned dome, its long spiral staircase and the ornate decorations and paintings surrounding Dona Maria's tomb all contribute to a truly aesthetic experience. Climb the 230 stairs to the church tower for a bird's-eye view of the city. Don't miss the church's beautiful gardens (Jardim da

*The lovely Jardin da Estrêla*

Estrêla) with their peacocks, ducks and geese strutting among the tropical plants.

This recently-renovated marble church is on the north-western side of Bairro Alto and can be reached by bus (no. 9 from Praça do Comércio; nos. 20 and 27 from Praça de Pombal) or by tram (nos. 25, 26, 28, 29, 30). The gardens are open until sunset. Entrance fee.

## The National Museum of Ancient Art (Museu Nacional de Arte Antiga)

Also called the "*Janelas Verdes*" ("Green Windows") after the street on which it stands, Portugal's National Museum is housed in an impressive 17th-century palace (the main entrance is from the new wing). Some of the most important and interesting works of art are on exhibit here, among them, wood statues by the Portuguese sculptor of the 18th century, Machado de Castro; silver pieces from Portugal and else-where, including a unique collection of 18th-century silver art from France; as well as a fine collection of European paintings by Raphael, Heironymus Bosch, Albrecht Durer, Hans Memling and Hans Holbein.

The Age of Discovery is well-represented here by a fine collection of 16th-century Japanese screens, an interesting Japanese perspective on the Portuguese arrival in Japan. Other impressive collections are the eastern-influenced Portuguese ceramics, and the porcelain brought back from India, Japan and Macau by Portuguese explorers.

A six-part polyptych entitled *Admiração de São Vicente*, by the 15th-century painter, Nuno Gonçalves, is the crowning jewel of the museum. It depicts Lisbon's patron saint surrounded by people from all levels of society – from the king, Dom Afonso V, to the commoner. The painter's image appears in the upper-lefthand corner of this masterpiece. Gonçalves's painting is part of a collection of 15th and 16th-century Portuguese painters.

You can get to the museum at 9, Rua das Janelas Verdes by bus (nos. 27 40 and 49) or by tram (no. 19). Open Tues.-Sun. 10am-1pm and 2:30-5pm; closed Mondays and holidays. Entrance fee; students and under 14 – free.

## The 25th of April Bridge (Ponte 25 de Abril)

Opened to traffic since 1966, this is one of the largest bridges in Europe. Over two kilometres long and 20 metres wide, the bridge rises seventy metres above the Tejo River. Thousands of vehicles cross the bridge daily on their way to and from the city. Initially called the **Ponte Sobre Tejo** (The Bridge above the Tejo), its name was changed to commemorate the start of the 1974 revolution. You can get to the bridge via Avenida da Ponte by taxi, by car or by bus (52 from the city centre).

*The 200m-high Cristo Rei*

The Almada and Cacilhas quarters are on the other side of the river. Coming from Lisbon, the 200m-high **Cristo Rei** statue is just on your left before the end of the bridge. This giant-sized statue was erected in 1959, and is a smaller model of the Corcovado that overlooks Rio de Janeiro in Brazil. The elevator inside this huge construction takes you up to one of the most wonderful views of the city. The **Church of Cristo Rei** is at the foot of the statue. An interesting way to get here is to take the ferry

*The 25th of April Bridge, connecting Belém to the quarters of Almada and Cacilhas*

across the river from Praça do Comércio to Cacilhas and catch the bus marked "Cristo Rei."

## Amoreiras Shopping Complex (Complexo das Amoreiras)

On the western side of Parque Eduardo VII is Lisbon's largest and most modern shopping centre. You can either walk to the Amoreiras Complex from the park via Rua Joaquim António de Aguiar which opens onto Avenida Duarte Pacheco, or by one of the many buses that go in that direction (11, 23, 53, and more).

The Amoreiras Shopping Complex was once a marketplace. During the 19th century the stalls were set up in the strawberry-tree gardens (Jardim das Amoreiras). With the recovery of Portugal's economy, a need arose for a large shopping and office complex. The complex of shops, offices and apartments covers 90,000 sq/m. and has 350 shops selling almost everything. Designed by Tomás Taveira, the complex is a most interesting architectural wonder. Taveira's aim was to create a city within a city. The complex gives the impression of a modern-day fortress or palace. The centre draws about 40,000 visitors each day, and the number of tickets sold in its ten cinemas is a quarter of all movie tickets sold throughout Portugal! The complex is open daily 8am to 11pm, and is indeed a shopper's paradise.

*The Amoreiras complex, Lisbon's most modern and attractive shopping center*

# AROUND LISBON

Outside Lisbon, Sintra, Cascais and Estoril are three main sites well worth a visit. There are, of course, other places to see, so leave enough time on your schedule to visit the castles, churches and tranquil fishing villages around Lisbon, as well as the beautiful beaches along the Atlantic coastline.

If you're going by car, the roads are all well-marked and there are plenty of picnic spots in wooded areas or on one of the many secluded beaches. With Lisbon as your base, you could take one of the following one or two-day trips. The tour guides in these regions are generally overly-eager to cover as much ground as possible.

If you're planning to travel outside the capital, there are two tours you should definitely consider. One is a day-tour to the Queluz and Sintra palaces, the Mafra Monastery, the Colares wine district and the Ericeira fishing village. The other route covers the Tejo River and the Atlantic coastline, and goes from Lisbon via Cascais and Estoril to the westernmost point on the continent, Cabo da Roca.

For those willing to travel 300km a day, there are also 2-day trips to Nazaré, via Óbidos in the north, and to Évora via Setúbal in the west.

*Inviting coastal scenery along the Atlantic coast near Lisbon – perfect for a soothing vacation*

## Accommodation

### ESTORIL

*Palácio*: Rua do Parque, Tel. 468 04 00, Fax 468 48 67. Famous five-star luxury hotel in beautiful park. Casino.

*Hotel Estoril Praia*: Avenida Marginal, Tel. 468 18 11, Fax 468 18 15. Four-star luxury hotel on coastal road.

*Hotel Paris*: Avenida Marginal, Tel. 468 00 18, Fax 467 11 71. Three-star hotel near casino.

### CASCAIS

*Hotel Estoril Sol*: Parque Palmela, Tel. 483 28 31, Fax 483 22 80. Five-star excellent hotel, frequented by Portuguese and foreign celebrities.

*Hotel Citadela*: Avenida 25 de Abril, Tel. 483 29 21, Beautiful four-star hotel with old-fashioned atmosphere.

Hotel Baía: Avenida Marginal, Tel. 483 10 33, Fax 483 10 95. Comfortable three-star hotel on the coastal road.

Village Cascais: Parque da Gandarinha, Tel. 483 70 44, Fax 483 73 19. Modern luxury hotel situated in a lovely park.

## AROUND LISBON

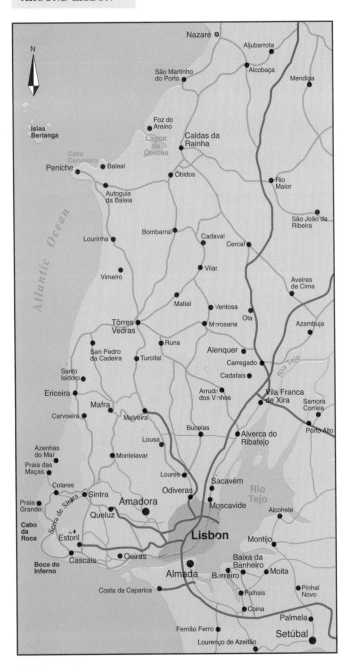

*Taking a brisk morning walk*

### SINTRA
Hotel Vale de Lobos: Vale de Lobos, Tel. 962 34 01, Fax 962 46 56. Three stars. Comfortable.

### ERICEIRA
Hotel Vilazul: 10, Calçada da Baleia, Tel. 86 41 01, Fax 86 29 27. Two stars. New hotel, nice and clean. Near the sea.

### SETÚBAL
Hotel Esperança: 220, Avenida Luisa Todi, Tel. 52 51 52.

Residencial Mare Sol: 606, Avenida Luisa Todi, Tel. 53 48 68. Private bath. Lovely view.

### ÉVORA
*Residencial Riviera*: 49, Rua 5 de Outubro, Tel. 2 33 04, Very comfortable four-star accomodation, near Praça do Giraldo. Bureau de change.

*Pensão Residencial o Ebornse*: 1, Largo de Misericórdia, Tel. 2 20 31, Three-star 16th-century manor. Charming setting.

### SPECIAL EVENTS

For the past 25 years, the Sintra Classical Music Festival has taken place between June and mid-July in the royal palaces of Queluz and Sintra. For further information and concert tickets call the tourist offices (*Tourismo*) in Sintra (Tel. 923 11 57) or Colares (Tel. 929 26 38), or you can call 923 48 45. Cascais hosts a Jazz Festival every summer; and at the race-track in nearby Estoril various car races are held throughout the year.

## Northwest of Lisbon — Queluz, Mafra and Ericeira

### Queluz — The Versailles of Lisbon

Lovers of Europe's ornate palaces will not want to miss the "Pink Palace" of Queluz. The town's name is from the Arabic "Vadi El Luz" meaning "Valley of the Almond Trees." Despite its Moorish name, and its ancient megaliths from the 3rd century BC,

*The magnificent interior of the Palace of Queluz*

the small town was of little significance until this Rococo palace was built in the 18th century. The palace's vast gardens are adorned with small ponds and marble statues (the palace and gardens are open to the public 10am-12.30pm and 2pm-5pm; and closed on Tuesdays. Entrance fee).

**Queluz** is only 14km outside of Lisbon and can be reached by train. Take the train to Sintra from the Rossio train station. The royal palace is to the south of the station: Turn left out of the station onto Avenida Antônio Enes; then continue along Avenida da República and Rua República to get to the palace.

The Royal Family was first brought to Queluz in 1747 by Dom Pedro VII, who was residing at the Marquês de Castelo Rodrigo's summer palace. The better part of the palace was built in 1758, and completed in 1760 when Dom Pedro married Dona Maria. Mateus Vicente de Oliveira and the Frenchman Jean-Baptiste Robillon, two leading artists of the day, supervised construction of the palace and

*Just back from a bus-trip, strolling along arm in arm*

the laying out of the gardens. The influence of the Palace at Versailles' is evident not only in the gardens but in the palace's baroque architecture, as well. Today, the palace is the Presidential summer home, and a guest-house for visiting dignitaries.

The **Throne Room** is the most impressive and lavish part of the palace. Its guilded walls and ceilings are decorated with paintings and wood carvings. The crystal chandeliers add the finishing touch to the room's imposing stateliness. The royal kitchen has been converted into a restaurant.

Take a walk in the splendid gardens, designed by Robillon and the Dutchman van der Kolk. Note the abundance of statues, fountains, and even a regal canal once used for sailing. The **Neptune Fountain** (Fonte de Neptuno) is said to have been made by the Italian, Bernini, the creator of many of Rome's beautiful fountains.

## Mafra –
## The Convent Memorial

In the heart of the small town of Mafra, 40km northwest of Lisbon, stands a huge monastery, **Convento de Mafra**, still inhabited by a small group of monks. You can get to Mafra via the N117 to Pero-Pinheiro and from there take the N9. An 80-minute bus ride leaves Lisbon from Largo Martim Moniz and from Rossio; or an hour-long bus ride leaves from the centre of Sintra. The monastery is open Wed.-Mon. 10am-5pm. Entrance fee. Try to come to Mafra during these hours, as the monastery is the town's main site of interest.

Mafra (like Lisbon) was conquered by the Moors in the mid-12th century. Life in this tranquil village was undisturbed until the 18th century. Dom João V, who had come to the throne in 1706, and his Austrian bride, María Ana, had been trying for two years to give birth to an heir. The king, renowned for his entanglements with the local nuns, was disturbed by rumours which reached the royal hearth and effected his wife's peace of mind. On a visit to his priest, the Franciscan monk António de São José, the king pledged to build a monastery in Mafra if his wish for an heir be granted. Less than a year later, the queen gave birth to Prince José, who in 1750 became king of Portugal, Dom José I.

Dom José, concerned with restoring the ruins of Lisbon after the 1755 earthquake, hardly frequented the monastery.

Besides the birth of an heir, other forces behind building of the Mafra Monastery were political interests and money. For over a century the Franciscans had striven to build a "strategic" monastery in the area, one that would serve as a Franciscan stronghold and overshadow the churches and monasteries of Portugal's monastic orders. It was a time of great wealth, and Brazilian gold was flowing into Dom João's royal treasury. The king sought to build a grand

*The huge and imposing monastery in Mafra has 2,000 rooms*

monument to celebrate his wealth and power, and looked to the Palace of Versailles and El Escorial in Madrid for inspiration. These motives, along with the king's desire for an heir, led to the construction of this fine monastery in 1717.

For 13 years, 50,000 workers (many of them forced laborers) toiled to erect the monastery. The German architect who designed the building, Friedrich Ludwig, eventually became a Portuguese citizen and changed his name to Ludovice. He and his son Peter are responsible for the Bavarian-looking towers guarding the front.

The monastery's proportions are particularly eccentric in Portugal's landscape of modest buildings. Large resources were put into the monastery: There is marble in most of the rooms and deer leather covers the furniture. The king's extravagance emptied the treasury and the building eventually became

*Picturesque Sintra*

a "white elephant." The palace (*Palácio*) on the monastery's grounds was hardly occupied by the royal family who preferred the palaces closer to the capital.

A visit to the 40,000 sq/m monastery (2,000 rooms, 5,200 doors, and about 2,500 windows) can be rather tiring.

Of particular interest is the basilica and its marble columns. Local artisans, under Italian supervision, working on marble from the nearby quarry, developed what became known as the Mafra School of Sculpture. The monastery's infirmary, no less fascinating than the other rooms, was built to allow patients to observe the mass from their beds. The library's collection of some 30,000 books is a priceless source of information for researchers and historians.

Every Sunday afternoon between 4-5pm the monastery's "bell concert" can be heard from far around. The 114 bells (about 50 in each tower) were made by *Lavache* in Antwerp. The heaviest bell weighs about 10 tons.

The Mafra Tourist Bureau is on Terreiro Dom João V, Tel. 061-81 21 21.

### FROM MAFRA TO ERICEIRA

The fishing village of Ericeira lies only 10km west of Mafra. You can get there by bus, or take the N116. A stop-over in **Sobreiro** and a visit to the studio of the sculptor José Franco is worthwhile. A gallery exhibits works in clay by the sculptor and his pupils, and there is also a miniature replica of rural Portugal. This is probably the last reminder of that 18th-century school of sculptors which developed at the time the monastery was being built.

Ericeira itself is a quiet friendly fishing village. The white houses on the harbour cliffs, the beautiful streets and clean beaches will make your stay here a pleasant one. The place used to be a favorite retreat for the Portuguese bourgeoisie in the 19th century and made the headlines in 1910, when Dom Manuel II, Portugal's last monarch, fled with his family to England in a yacht from here.

Take the opportunity for a fine seafood meal at a local restaurant before heading back to Lisbon.

## Sintra – Glorious Eden

Lord Byron's words of praise for Sintra – "Lo! Cintra's glorious Eden intervenes in variegated maze of mount and glen" – have become something of a cliché in almost all tourist brochures. Without resorting to trite superlatives, Sintra is indeed "breathtakingly beautiful"! This cool green resort is a splendid place to visit during the hot summer months. During the transitional seasons you'll need warm clothing. Even from the relatively low (530m) Sintra mountain range (**Serra de Sintra**), you can feel the effect of the Atlantic Ocean on the climate.

Sintra lies about 30km west of Lisbon. Take

the N249 if you have a car, or any of the regular trains leaving from Rossio in central Lisbon. Look out for the aqueduct (on the left going to Sintra) if you're taking the train.

It's best *not* to visit Sintra on Mondays when the royal castle is closed; nor on Tuesdays – the Pena Palace is closed to the public. The colorful **Feira de São Pedro** market is held every second and fourth Sunday of the month, and offers almost anything for sale. The forests and hillsides outside the village are lusciously green with cedars, pines, tropical and subtropical plants and trees. Exploring the surrounding area on foot is not only an historical, but a purely "natural" experience.

Our tour of Sintra focuses on its castles and palaces, but don't forgo a casual stroll through the town's picturesque sidestreets. Our tour begins at the **City Square** (Cámara Municipal) with its mixture of architectural styles. From the City Square (near the railway station), take the winding gravel road through the park to the **National Palace** (Palácio Nacional de Sintra, otherwise known as the Paço de Villa or Paço Real, the Royal Palace). The palace's large

chimneys make it particularly visible on the hillside. Well-kept gardens and fountains line the palace grounds. A detailed guidebook of the area can be bought at the tourist bureau near the palace. Open daily between 8am-8pm, Tel. 923 11 57. The **Church of São Martinho** (Igreja de São Martinho) is also at this site.

From as early as the 15th century, the National Palace served as a royal fortress and retreat during the hot summer months. The course marked out for visitors covers most of the palace's interesting rooms. For almost two centuries new wings were added to the palace; its unusual exterior is the result of the changing architectural styles. The route takes you up and down countless stairways and along the palace's narrow and winding corridors (Open Tues.-Sun. 10am-1pm and 2.30pm-5pm; closed Monday. Tickets can be bought until 30 minutes before closing time).

The palace was built towards the end of the 14th century by Dom João I on the ruins of an ancient Moorish castle. The entrance is through the stone arches and the stairway in the front. Afonso V and João II built the front in the 15th century to fortify the palace. The next stop is the Gothic-styled

palace kitchens with their old cooking utensils and antique kitchen furniture. This is also where the large chimneys in the front originate.

From here, the tour takes you to the various bedrooms for an impression of day-to-day life in the palace after it was expanded and renovated in the 16th century by Manuel I. Canopy beds, weaving looms and period furniture are scattered throughout these bedrooms, which lead onto the beautiful chapel. Standing on the balcony at the top of the stairs, you can get a closer look at the chapel's Arab-style ceiling. The floor is covered in maginificent ceramic tiles depicting intricate scenes. From the chapel continue to the treasure room and its collection of ivory from the Far East. In the adjoining room Afonso VI was imprisoned by his brother for nine years until his death in 1683. Dom Pedro II believed his brother insane and induced him to step down from the thrown; he later married his brother's wife.

Other stops on the guided tour are the **Shield Room** (Sala dos Brasões) proudly exhibiting the coats-of-arms of the Portuguese nobility; the Manueline-style **Arab Room** (Sala dos Arabes) with its ancient and rare colored tiles; and the ceiling of the **Magpie Room** (Sala das Pegas), painted with 136 magpies each with the inscription "Por Bem" ("for the good") beneath it. This is where Queen Philippa of Lancaster caught her husband, Dom João I, kissing one of her ladies-in-waiting. When confronted by the queen, the king gave his motive: "Por Bem" – "for the good." To please the queen and to avoid jeopardizing Anglo-Portuguese relations, the king had the ceiling painted with "gossiping" magpies, equal in number to the queen's ladies-in-waiting.

The Sintra palace is situated on the green slopes of the Cruz Alta mountain, 529m above sea-level. Don't miss the **Pena Palace** (Palácio da Pena) on the mountain top. You can either get to the top by car, taxi, or climb the 4km winding road.

The **Moorish Castle** (Castelo dos Mouros) on the way up is covered today by forest. The North African Moors, spreading Islam and its culture, built a strong fortress here and ruled the coastline in the 8th and 9th centuries. Due to slack military discipline and internal strife among the Moorish tribes, this enclave gradually grew weaker, and the

*The faded yet lovely colors of the Pena Palace*

*The Pena Palace looks as if it had come right out of a fairy-tale book*

Christian forces under Afonso Henriques met with no resistance when capturing the abandoned fortress in 1147. The first Christian monarchs added a chapel and built more rooms, but in time they too abandoned the castle. Open from 9am to sunset. Entrance free.

From the castle walls there's a scenic view of the green Sintra mountain range.

### PENA PALACE (PALÁCIO DA PENA)

Sitting on the mountain peak, Palácio da Pena was the home of Dona Maria I and her beloved husband Ferdinand of Saxony.

The palace is built on the ruins of a 16th-century monastery, destroyed in the 1755 earthquake. The royal couple built the palace 150 years ago, blending Gothic, Manueline, Moorish and Renaissance styles. The palace interior is just as surprising and non-uniform as its exterior. Don't miss the large dome, the clock-tower, the beautiful balcony on the cliff, and the palace's magnificent gardens (Open Wed.-Mon. 10am-6pm, closed Tuesdays. Tickets are sold until 30 minutes from closing time).

From the top of **Cruz Alta** (the High Cross)

there's an excellent view of Lisbon and the Estoril coastline. Those wishing to explore the region further, can visit **Seteais Palace**, now a hotel to the west of Sintra, and various other rural churches.

Since the Christian conquest of the 12th century, a village fair has been held on the second and fourth Sunday of every month in the neighboring São Pedro village. You can find, besides the usual souvenirs, good country cheese and bread, original handicrafts, ancient tools, coins, and much more.

## Colares

This romantic village lies 7km west of Sintra. The small village and its vineyards stretch across two beautiful hills on the Sintra range. Excellent wine has been manufactured here for thousands of years.

The Romans were probably the first to plant vines here, and even after they left the wine-making legacy remained. In the 12th and 13th centuries Dom Afonso II encouraged the wine industry by giving land to the vine-growers in exchange for a regular supply of wine to the court. The superb *Ramisco* grapes, brought to the region in the 13th

century, flourished in the moderate and wet climate. Because the Colares region is relatively small and the quality of the produce so high, the wines have become rare and much sought-after. A visit to one of the vineyards, such as *Tavares & Rodrigues* provides a good opportunity to taste and purchase some of these fine wines.

## Estoril and Cascais – A Journey to the Atlantic Shores

On the coastline west of Lisbon lie the capital's centres of sun and fun – beaches, bustling streets and colorful fish restaurants are the main pastimes here.

The N6 out of Lisbon heads westward to Estoril, 30km from the capital; and 3km further on to Cascais. A 30-minute express bus ride links Lisbon with Estoril and Cascais, yet the best way to get there is by train (*comboio*). There are regular trains from the Cais do Sodré train station near Praça do Comércio in central Lisbon. The train travels along the shores of the Tejo River and the Atlantic Ocean. These beaches are polluted and not fit for bathing. Cascais is the train's last stop on this coastal ride, commonly known as "The Marginal Route" (**Estrada Marginal**).

Leaving the Cais do Sodré train station the journey takes you past Belém (see "Belém – The Jewel of the Sea") and along the Tejo River. At the **Dáfundo** station, near **Algés**, is the **Vasco da Gama Aquarium** (Aquário Vasco da Gama) with an inter-

seting display of fish and sea plants. The aquarium opened about a century ago, celebrating 400 years since Vasco da Gama's voyage to India. Recommended for children and lovers of the silent underwater world (open Mon.-Sat. and holidays, 12pm-6pm; Sundays 10am-6pm. Entrance fee).

The train route follows the river until **Oeiras**, 10km west of Lisbon, where the Atlantic beaches begin. This coastline, previously known as **Costa do Sol** ("The Sun Coast), is now called **Costa do Estoril**. Tranquil Oeiras is itself an interesting town which once belonged to the Oeiras nobleman, the Marquês de Pombal, the famous restorer of Lisbon after the 1755 earthquake. Of particular interest is the Marquês' 18th-century palace (*Palácio*) with its ornate ceilings, and his collection of paintings, furniture and household tools. The palace also has beautiful gardens and a wine cellar where the Marquês produced his own wine (Open Wed.-Mon. 10am-6pm. Entrance fee.)

The **Bugio lighthouse** facing Oeiras was built in 1755 in the shape of a small fortress as a signal to guide ships entering the mouth of the Tejo. The train stops next at Carcavelos, known for its good beaches. This is also where the underwater telephone line to the Azores Islands begins.

## Estoril

The train stops at Estoril station near the well-known crowded Tamariz beach. For the past centuries, Estoril has been the home of Portugal's rich and famous who seek its beaches, green landscapes and unique ambience. Among the many who once lived here are King Umberto of Italy and King Juan Carlos of Spain, who spent his childhood days here.

The main attractions in Estoril are its casino (**Casino Estoril**) and the beautiful park (**Parque Estoril**) fronting it. The country's most lavish casino is open daily from 3pm to the early hours of the morning, except for Christmas and Easter Friday (*Sexta-Feira Santa*). You'll find the regular card and roulette tables, as well as the customary one-arm bandits. There are also Las Vegas-style shows and lavish dinners (dinners begin at 8.30pm, the shows – at 11.15pm. Tel. 468 45 21 for reservations). Around the park, blooming with red and lilac bougainvillea, you'll find hotels, restaurants and a race-track (**Autodromio**), as well as

*Enjoying the sun on the beach at Cascais*

tennis courts, golf-courses and swimming pools for those who want to pay for a luxury holiday.

*an exquisite garden in bloom at Cascais*

The Estoril Tourist Bureau is on Arcadas do Parque, Tel. 468 01 13.

## Cascais

It was once said of this fishing village "A Cascais uma vez e nunca mais" ("Once to Cascais, and never again"). What was once considered a distant and somewhat dormant village, is now a bustling tourist centre.

This transformation is mainly due to Dom Carlos (1889-1908), a sea-loving admiral, who settled in Cascais. A new road was built to the village, which began drawing the literati and glitterati of Lisbon: artists, aristocracy and rich businessmen. Cascais is no longer a quiet fishing village, but a charming district near Lisbon with a character of its own.

The village is still inhabited by fishermen, who have been living here for centuries. Fishing boats and travellers haul in their catch under a cloud of eager and hungry seagulls. The fish and seafood are taken immediately to the fish market, later to be served in the village's excellent sea-food restaurants.

**City Hall** (Paço do Conselho) is on the main square, and decorated with steel lattices and ceramic tile scenes. The 17th-century **Citadel** (Citadela) survived the earthquake in the 18th century and later became Dom Carlos' residence. The **Guimarães Museum**, on Count Castro Guimarães' property, has an interesting collection of paintings, statues, and gold and silver pieces. The museum is in Gandarinha park, and is open Thurs.-Sun. 10am-6pm (Entrance fee).

The main attraction of any visit to Cascais is a stroll along the coast and the pedestrian malls in between the houses and churches. A new promenade and quay were built after the flood of 1984 destroyed most of the beachfront.

The Cascais Tourist Bureau is on Praça 5 de Outubro, Tel. 484 64 44.

## The Coastline

From the market in Cascais we go west along the coastal road. A short distance up the road is **Boca do Inferno** ("Inferno's Jaw") where the waves pounding the cliffs have created a huge hole through which the water shoots 20m into the air. It's worth stopping to watch the spray and hear the loud noise coming from this "jaw of hell."

The quieter beaches of **Praia do Guincho** are several kilometres further along the coastal road.

At Cabo da Roca nearby, the Sintra range ends with a 150m cliff above the sea. This is the westernmost point of Europe,

*At the Cascais beach – a wave to the ship at sea*

and you can purchase an official document to prove you've been here.

From here, you can either continue on to Sintra or return to Lisbon. Travelling by car is the most convenient way to get to the end of the continent and its beautiful beaches. A bus leaves every 40 minutes from the train station in Cascais to Cabo da Roca from 8am-8pm, or else you can take the bus from Sintra.

# DAY TOURS

For those willing to travel 150km out of Lisbon, there are some wonderful sites to visit. There are two suggested day-long routes. Be sure to make an early start if you want to take in all the recommended spots.

Going northwards from Lisbon, the first route takes you via Óbidos to Alcobaça and Nazaré. The second trip goes eastward to Setúbal and Évora. Visiting these beautiful sites can be very rewarding and make the lengthy journeys well worthwhile.

### Route 1 – Lisbon-Óbidos-Alcobaça-Nazaré

The "high road" – A8 – goes from Lisbon to Óbidos (via Tôrres Vedras and Bombarral), but it's better to take the "low roads", which might be slower, but offer magical landscapes and picturesque villages along the way. The train to Óbidos leaves from Rossio station.

#### ÓBIDOS

About 95km north of Lisbon, Óbidos is a charming village with a population of 5,000. One of Portugal's gems, this village has enchanted many throughout history. Dom Dinis gave the village to his wife Isabella, and for 550 years (until 1832) it was passed down from monarch to monarch.

*An enthusiastic traveller*

An 18th-century ceramic tile (*azulejos*) gateway welcomes those entering Óbidos. Many of ancient Óbidos' narrow streets are closed to traffic, so it's best to park your car outside the gate.

The walls around Óbidos were first built by the Moors and later restored in the Middle Ages. Take the stairway at the entrance to climb the walls; the view from the top is worth the effort.

The impressive medieval fortress on the northern side of the walls later became a royal palace, part of which is now a

9-room *pousada* (a government-owned hotel in an historical site). Expensive; reservations must be made in advance (Tel. 062-95 91 05).

From the fortress we go down to Rua Direita, Óbidos' main street, with its many souvenir shops and a tourist office. Further along the Rua Direita is the **Church of Santa Maria** (Igreja de Santa Maria), where Dom Afonso V and his cousin Isabel were married in 1444 when still children. The church has an ornamental ceiling and 17-century tile panels on the walls. On most days you can watch artists at work outside the church.

Óbidos' narrow and winding alleyways take you through this colorful vilage: the white, blue and yellow houses, and the window-boxes filled with geraniums and bougainvillea paint a beautiful picture.

The Óbidos Tourist Bureau is on Solar da Praça de Santa Maria, Tel. 062-95 92 96.

### FROM ÓBIDOS TO ALCOBAÇA
Travelling north from Óbidos, we get to the spa-town of **Caldas da Rainha**, where its 16,000 inhabitants depend on the spa and hot springs for their livelihood.

The name Caldas da Rainha means "The Queen's Spa" and dates back to Dona Leonor who passed through in 1484 and noticed the locals bathing in the sulphur baths. Impressed by the spa's medicinal powers, the Queen built a hospital here offering unique treatments.

Continuing along the N8 we get

*Fishermen with their haul*

to Alfeizerão. If you want to stop for lunch on the beachfront, turn left on the N242 to Nazaré; to continue the tour, go on to Alcobaça, further along the N8.

A small village with a population of 5,000, Alcobaça is famous for the **Abadia Real de Santa Maria** – the largest monastery in Portugal. This grand monastery was built by Afonso I in 1148 after the Moors were defeated at **Santarém**. The front door and window are all that remain of the original monastery; the rest was rebuilt and renovated during the 17th and 18th centuries.

The monastery houses the tombs of the legendary and tragic lovers, Dom Pedro I and Inês de Castro. When in 1340 Afonso IV married off his son, Pedro, to Constance of Castile, she brought with her her lady-in-waiting, Inês de Castro. Pedro fell madly in love with the beautiful Inês and had her sent to a nunnery, where she gave birth to four of his children. When Queen Constance died in 1345, Inês and the young Pedro were secretly wed. The king objected to the marriage, and had Inês killed in 1355. Two years later, when Pedro became king, he had Inês exhumed, dressed her in the royal gown, and sat her on the throne. In a macabre ceremony, the courtiers and noblemen were made to kiss what remained of her hand. The body was subsequently reinterred, and when he died, Pedro I was buried facing his love. These Gothic tombs were mildly damaged during the French invasion of 1811.

### NAZARÉ

Nazaré lies 11km from Alcobaça and about 30km from Caldas da Rainha. The town was named after the statue of the Virgin Mary, brought from Nazareth in the 4th century (the statue is no longer here).

Follow the signposts marked **Sítio** or **Mirador** or take the cable-car to the cliff-top Sítio quarter. This 110m-high cliff overlooks the multitude of tents set up by holidaymakers on the beach, the gay fishing boats and the locals in traditional dress complete the colorful backdrop. Going down to the **Praia** ("beach") quarter you'll smell the grilled sardines (*sardinhas*) sizzling on the coals.

There is no shortage of souvenir shops in Nazaré, selling handmade jerseys, porcelain and cork and textile products at much cheaper prices than in Lisbon.

To get back to Lisbon, you can return either the way we came (via the N242 and then back onto the N8); or, even better, take the coastal road. Although much slower and somewhat longer, the scenery is far nicer.

The Tourist Bureau in Nazaré is on Avenida da República. Tel. 062-56 11 94.

## Route 2 – Lisbon-Setúbal-Évora

### SETÚBAL

The A2 will get you to Setúbal, 50km south-east of Lisbon, on the northern shore of the Sado River, at the foot of the Arrábida mountains. The town's 6,000 inhabitants depend largely on the port, industry and tourism for their livelihood. The bus to Setúbal (and to Évora) leaves from Praça de Espanha, and the train to Setúbal leaves from the Barreiro train station on the south side of the Tejo River.

Setúbal, the third largest port in Portugal after Lisbon and Porto, is used mainly for hauling in catches of sardines and cultivating oysters (*camarão*). Although considered a delicacy by the Portuguese, most of the oysters are exported to European countries.

If you arrive by car, it's best to park near Praça Almirante Reis, and take a short stroll around the city's old quarter, ending up at the **Igreja de Santa Maria**.

The Tourist Bureau in Setúbal is on Largo do Corpo Santo. Tel. 065-24284.

### ÉVORA

Take the eastbound N10 from Setúbal, continue along route 11, and at the junction with route 44 turn right. At Montemor-o-Novo continue along the N114 until Évora.

*A blend of architectural styles in Évora*

Évora has a population of 45,000 and is the capital of the province of **Alto Alentejo**. A visit to Évora is a journey back in time: The town is a mixture of Roman architecture, Moorish sidestreets, and grand medieval and Renaissance palaces.

Although you can get to the city centre (Praça do Giraldo) by car, parking is a problem and it's best to use the lot facing Rua da República. A guide to the city is available from the Tourist Bureau on 1 Rua 24 de Julho, Tel. 066-74 25 35.

The **Church of São Francisco**

(Igreja de São Francisco) on Rua da República is one of the more interesting and curious sites in Évora, if not in the entire region. This typically Manueline-Gothic church is adorned with tiles (*azulejos*) and marble. The walls and pillars of the macabre 16th-century chapel are lined with some 5,000 skulls and bones. A winding corridor leads the way to this House of Bones (**Casa dos Ossos**). There is no entrance charge to the church; to get into the chapel you'll need to pay a small fee. Open 7.30am-1pm and 2.30pm-8pm; in winter until 5pm. Leaving the church, turn onto Traversa, the picturesque main street, and then onto Rua dos Mercadores, which leads to the town square, **Praça do Giraldo**.

Turn onto the colorful Rua 5 de Outubro, commemorating the 1910 revolution, with its old houses and heavy iron bars above the souvenir and handicraft stores. Prices are much lower here than in Lisbon. At the end of the street, the cluster of beautiful buildings includes the **Sé**, a Romano-Gothic cathedral built in 1186, using a 18th-century Neo-classical chapel and a small museum. Two tall towers add the finishing touches to the cathedral's sombre façade. The **Évora Museum** (Museu de Évora), to the left of the cathedral, was the local bishop's palatial home in the 16th century. The museum has collections of Portuguese and Flemmish paintings, statues, furniture and ornaments.

Further on are the remains of **Diana's Temple**, known also as the **Roman Temple** (Templo Romano). This small Corinthian temple was built in the 2nd or 3rd century AD, when Évora was a Roman town, *Liberalitas Julia*. The temple may have been dedicated to the goddess Diana, and was probably only part of a larger construction. In medieval times the temple was transformed into a fortress, and later used (until 1870) as a slaughterhouse. The temple's capitals and base are marble; the pillars are granite.

To the right, east of the temple, is a group of Gothic-Mudéjar buildings. Mudéjar is a Moorish architectural style which evolved during the Christian conquest. Many Moslem architects, artisans and builders were detained by the Christians to erect glorious buildings for the Christian monarchs. In 1390, Dom José gave one of these buildings, the Paço dos Duques de Cadaval, as a gift to his adviser. The northern side of the palace also serves as part of the city's walls, originally built in the Middle Ages and renewed in the 17th century. There is a display of historical documents belonging to the Cadaval family in the palace's gallery. Open 10am-12.30pm and 2pm-5pm. Closed on Mondays and holidays.

The route continues via Rua de Serra da Tourega to Rua Misericórdia and Rua M. Bombarda, and then back to the Praça do Giraldo and the 16-century **Church of Santo Antão**. Take a break at one of the local cafés before heading back, via Rua da República, to the parking lot.

*Enjoy the soft sand and calm waters of Portugal's beaches*

# "MUSTS"

Lisbon has a lot to offer. To make sure you don't miss out on the important sites, we've prepared a list of "musts" in and around the capital. If you intend staying for only a short while, we recommend you follow these suggestions:

**São Jorge Castle** (Castelo de São Jorge) – On the hilltop overlooking central Lisbon and the Tejo River. Beautiful views, lovely gardens and many varieties of birds.

**Rossio Square** – Lisbon's main square. Cafés, the National Theatre, a small flower market, railway station and more.

**City Centre – Baixa** – The "low quarter", Baixa lies south of Rossio. The quarter was rebuilt after the 1755 earthquake by the Marquês de Pombal. The criss-crossing streets of Baixa are lined with lively cafés, shops and street markets. You'll also find the Santa Justa elevator here, and much more.

*A splendidly decorated building in Bairro Alto*

**Alfama Quarter** – This charming and vibrant neighborhood is the city's oldest. Since the Middle Ages, these narrow and winding streets have been home to Lisbon's fishermen and laborers.

**Chiado** – The main square in Bairro Alto; once the elegant culture centre of 18th-century Lisbon. Unique cafés and beautiful shops.

**The Carmo Monastery** (Igreja do Carmo) – The roof of this Carmelite church caved in during the earthquake and was never repaired. Today, it houses an archeological museum. In Bairro Alto.

**Belém** – The western quarter of Lisbon. Its main attractions are the **Monastery of Jerónimos** (Mosteiro dos Jerónimos), the **National Coach Museum** (Museu dos Coches) and the **Tower of Belém** (Torre de Belém).

**The National Museum of Ancient Art** (Museu Nacional de Arte Antiga) – A fascinating museum with rare collections of art from Portugal's long history, as well as collections from voyages of discovery dating back to the 15th century.

**The Church of Madre de Deus** – One of the city's richest and most beautiful monasteries. Houses the **Tile Museum** (Museu dos Azulejos) as well.

## Around Lisbon

**Sintra** – A green mountain ridge 30km northwest of Lisbon, with luxurious palaces and wonderful scenery.

**Estoril** – A charming holiday village on the Atlantic coast, home to the country's most renowned casino.

*At the National Coach Museum, housing one of the finest collections of coaches in the world*

**Cascais** – Once a quiet fishing village, now a favorite resort for artists and the rich.

# MAKING THE MOST OF YOUR STAY

## Portuguese Cuisine

According to a popular saying, *Não há feste sem comer*, or freely translated, "there's no celebration without food." In Lisbon, the locals abide by this rule. The rich Portuguese kitchen makes abundant use of olive oil, initially introduced by the Moors, and of the cinammon, vanilla and pepper, brought home from afar by the great explorers.

Unlike French or Belgian cuisine, Portuguese cooking is not sophisticated or delicate, but no less interesting and deli-

*Portuguese cooking is often characterized by sea-food*

cious. Based mainly on fish and seafood, the methods of preparation are numerous, the portions big, and the ingredients rich. If you're concerned about calories and cholesterol, the Portuguese might tell you that *Quem bem come e bebe, faz o que deve* ("he who eats and drinks properly, functions properly").

*Caldo verde*, "green soup," is a typical Portuguese **soup** (*sopa*). Made from cabbage and mashed potatoes, this soup is sometimes served with pork sausages (*chouriço*). "Portuguese soup," *sopa à Portuguesa*, is similar in taste, with the addition of carrots, cauliflower, beans and other ingredients. Pea soup, *sopa de grão*, is also very tasty. *Sopa de cozido* is a rich soup made with meat and macaroni, and may suffice as a main course.

**Fish** (*peixe*) and **seafood** (*mariscos*) dominate the main courses. The local favorite, codfish (*bacalhau*), is not

caught off the coast, but brought in from afar. There are dozens of ways to prepare codfish, the most popular being the *bacalhau à Brás* – a mixture of puréed fish and potatoes cooked in olive oil, egg, onions and garlic. Another favorite is the *bacalhau à gomes de sá*, pieces of skinned and boned fish baked with milk and potatoes. This delicacy is usually served with a hard-boiled egg and olives, and is worth a try.

Another fish and seafood dish is the *caldeirada à fragateira*, a rich fish soup eaten as a main course. *Açorda* is a thick and filling egg-drop soup with seafood and bread. Something else worth tasting is *lulas recheadas* (calamari with rice, vegetables and spices), and also *lagosta suada* (fried lobster, marinated in garlic, tomatoes, onions and port), *atum* (tuna in different varieties) and *arroz*, rice cooked with seafood (a distant cousin of the Spanish *paella*).

Among the favorite **meats** here are beef (*bife*), goat (*cabrito*), pork (*porco*), prepared either roasted (*assado*), charcoal-grilled (*grelhado*), fried (*frito*) or boiled (*cozido*).

Most restaurants serve the popular *cozido à Portuguesa* – beef and pork boiled in a pot with cabbage, potatoes, rice, salami, etc. The beef in a pan, *bife na frigideira*, is the local steak often prepared in a delicious wine sauce. Many restaurants also serve *feijoada*, a thick Brazilian stew of beans and pork, lovingly adopted by the Portuguese.

Lisbon is a dessert-lover's heaven. The huge variety of sweet **desserts** (*sobremesa*) range from sweet rice pudding (*arroz doce*) or caramel flan (*pudim flan*) served in the workers' restaurants, to the more delicate desserts which

originated in the city's monasteries. What was created by the nuns over the centuries, can now be ordered in most of the better restaurants: "Nun's belly" (*barriga de freira*), "angel's cheeks" (*papos de anjo*) and an egg sweet called *doce de ovos* are only three of many. Be warned that Portuguese desserts tend to be much sweeter than anywhere else. Consider the full selection before you choose!

Portugal's famous **port** also deserves a mention. Don't miss out on a taste of this lustrous wine when in its land of origin.

Here is a short list of restaurants. Lunch is usually served between 12.30pm-3pm, and dinner between 7-10pm.

## BAIXA

Rua das Portas de Santo Antão in Baixa is known for its seafood restaurants; worth mentioning are the *Escorial* at no. 47 (Tel. 346 44 29), *Lagosta Real* at no. 37 (Tel. 342 39 95), *Solmar* at no. 108 (Tel. 342 33 71), and *Marisqueira da Baixa* at no. 41 (Tel. 342 78 67).

*Bonjardim*: 11, Travessa de Santo Antão, Tel. 342 74 24. Excellent chicken dishes.

*An assorted array of tasty desserts*

*A fado performance, full of soul and sentiment*

*Uma*: 117, Rua dos Sapateiros, Tel. 342 74 25.

### BAIRRO ALTO

*Cervejaria da Trindade*: 20-C, Rua Nova da Trindade, Tel. 342 35 06. Portuguese cuisine, mainly fish and seafood. Tile decorations. Reasonable prices.

*Bachus*: 9, Largo da Trindade, Tel. 32 28 28. Meat. Expensive.

*Tavares Rico*: 35-37, Rua da Misericórdia, Tel. 342 11 12. Luxurious restaurant, superb cooking.

*Aviz*: 12-B, Rua Serpa Pinto, Tel. 342 83 91. Luxurious. International menu.

*Canto do Camões*: 38, Travessa da Espera, Tel. 346 54 64. Good food and fado performances.

*Casa Transmontana*: 39, Calçada do Duque, Tel. 342 03 00. Portuguese cuisine. Reasonable prices.

*Bota Alta*: 35, Travessa da Queimada, Tel. 342 79 59. Popular and cheap.

*A Colmeira*: 110, Rua da Emenda, Tel. 347 05 00. Vegetarian.

*Adega Machado*: 91, Rua
do Norte, Tel. 342 87 13.
Reasonable prices.

## ALFAMA
*Mestre André*: 6, Calçadinha
de Santo Estêvão, Tel.
397 79 98. Superb.
Brazilian music.

*Dragão de Alfama*: 8, Rua
Guilherme Braga, Tel.
886 77 37. Near the Church of
Santo Estêvão. Portuguese
cuisine.

## BELÉM
*Vela Latina*: Doca do Bom
Sucesso, Tel. 301 71 18.
Superb. Portuguese cuisine,
pleasant atmosphere.
Air-conditioned. Reasonable
prices.

*Montenegro*: 44, Rua Vieira
Portuense, Tel. 363 82 79.
Superb.

*Sagitário*: 10/2, Rua de Belém,
Tel. 364 56 87.

The following restaurants are
also recommended:

*Casa do Leão*: Castelo do
São Jorge, Tel. 87 59 62.
Luxurious and air-conditioned.
Fine view of the city.
Open daily, afternoons
only.

*Varina da Madragoa*: 36,
Rua das Madres Santos, Tel.
396 55 33. Near Lisbon's
Parliament. Portuguese
cuisine. Simple and
pleasant.

*Coelho Dourado*: 101, Avenida
Conde de Valbom, Tel.
797 06 88. Near Gulbenkian
Foundation. Portuguese.

*Gondola*: 64, Avenida de
Berna, Tel. 797 04 26. Near
Gulbenkian Foundation.
Expenisve.

*Splendid decor at Cervejaria da Trindade*

*Campo Pequeno*: 76/9, Campo Pequeno, Tel. 793 97 60. Inexpenisve.

*O Madeirense*: Amoreiras Shopping Complex, Tel. 69 08 27. Portuguese cuisine.

## AROUND PARQUE EDUARDO VII

*Li Yuan*: 23-A/B, Rua Viriato, Tel. 57 77 40. Chinese.

*Hong Kong*: 23-B, Rua Camilo Castelo Branco, Tel. 353 86 65. Chinese.

# Filling the Basket: Where to Shop for What?

As in any big city, there are plenty of shops, so you needn't worry if you've forgotten to bring something with you. Be it a battery or a video camera. In general, electrical appliances and imported computers cost the same as in most European cities. The real bargains are the handicrafts and locally-made products. Since Lisbon is one of the cheapest capitals in the EEC, prices can differ immensely throughout the city. It is best, therefore, to compare prices before purchasing. Portugal also has a simple and effective system of refunding VAT (see below) which makes the purchase much less expensive (not true in the case of electric appliances).

Local markets are the best place to find embroidered maps, wool and cotton knitwear, Alentejo rugs, hand-painted wooden cocks, decorated tiles, woven baskets and other ceramic and porcelain handicrafts. Portugal is also the largest manufacturer of cork products. Clothes are inexpensive, although styles are somewhat behind the rest of western Europe. Leather goods, particularly leather bags, are cheaper here. When it comes to wines, even the finest of Portugal's wines are relatively cheap.

The many antique shops offer antiques related somehow to the city's past. The risk buying here is twofold: you'll feel cheated if you buy a fake for the price of an original; and, if it is an original, you'll have trouble getting it out of the country without the necessary permits. Make sure you ask the store-owner for the relevant permit. It's much less troublesome to buy porcelain or gold and silver jewelery, still designed in keeping with the tradition that evolved during the Moorish invasion over 1,000 years ago.

Since Lisbon was, until recently, the centre of a vast colonial power, you'll come

*Browsing around the market of Feira da Ladra*

across a large selection of art and handicrafts from its former colonies in Africa and the Far East at very reasonable prices.

The capital's main shopping areas are central Lisbon, Baixa, the city's traditional shopping centre; the larger and newer shops along the Avenida da Liberdade; and also the modern shopping complex, Complexo das Amoreiras, west of Praça Marquês de Pombal. Avid shoppers familiarize themselves with the variety of shops by wandering through the city streets (see the routes listed as "Baixa – The Heart of the City" and "The Greenfields of Lisbon – From Praça dos Restauradores to Parque Eduardo VII"). There are also a variety of interesting shops in other parts of the city, such as the Chiado.

Antique-lovers will want to visit Rua Dom Pedro V, and the adjoining Rua de São Pedro de Alcântara to the south, and Rua da Escola Politécnica to the north. Visiting many of these shops is an experience in itself.

If you're looking for decorated tiles (you can have them made on request) the best places to shop are on Rua da Escola Politécnica, as well as Rua do João (near the Amoreiras shopping centre) and on Rua do Alecrim in Bairro Alto.

If you're shopping for aquarels, Rua Augusta in Baixa is where you'll find them. There are many silver and gold shops on Rua do Ouro and Rua da Prata.

## Tax Refunds

Tourists from outside the EEC are entitled to tax refunds on their purchases, providing they were bought at authorized

*An ornamented store in Bairro Alto*

shops and are worth over $100 (local currency; in one purchase, not including tax). The shops selling tax-refundable goods are marked with green and red stickers – "*Tax free for tourists*". All of Lisbon's expensive and exclusive shops have this permit.

After you've made the purchase, the salesperson will fill out a cheque with your personal details (carry a passport with you) and details of the purchase. When leaving the country, you must present the goods and the cheque at customs. Once they have been approved, your VAT will be refunded in cash (in escudos) at the counter marked with the same green and red sticker. You can also send the cheque to the address printed on it from your home, and have the tax refund sent to you directly, or refunded through your credit card.

The amount refunded differs according to the tax on each product; it is generally between 10% and 15%, but may also reach 20%. You can get the tax refund at Lisbon Airport (near Gate 24 in the departure lounge), at Lisbon Harbor (next to customs), and at all other airports in Portugal. Those leaving Portugal by train or car will have to send the cheque by mail (for further information call Tel. 418 87 03).

There's a Duty-Free shop on 50, Rua Latino Coelho (Tel. 355 92 96).

## A Selection of the City's Shops

### DEPARTMENT STORES
*Pollux*: 276, Rua dos Fanqueiros. Tel. 886 97 44.

*A Loja*: 229, Rua da Prata. Tel. 342 76 67. Leather (*Artigos a Confecções em Pele*).

*Darny*: 67, Rua do Carmo. Tel. 346 79 05.

*Adão Camiseiros*: 238-240, Rua Augusta. Tel. 346 61 18.

*Authentik*: 34, Avenida da Roma (other branches on Rossio and Complexo das Amoreiras).

### EMBROIDERY (*BORDADO*)
*Casa dos Bordados Reginal da Madeira*: Jardim do Regedor (near Praça dos restauradores). Tel. 346 83 35.

*Casa Regional da Ilha Verde*: 4, Rua Paiva Andrade (Chiado). Tel. 342 59 74.

*Madeira Supérbia*: 88, Rua

*Complexo das Amoreiras*

Rodrigo da Fonseca (inside the *Ritz Hotel*). Tel. 388 05 48.

### REGIONAL HANDICRAFTS (*ARTESANATO E ARTIGOS REGIONAIS*)
*Artesanato Arameiro dos Restauradoes*: 62, Praça dos Restauradores. Tel. 342 02 36.

*Amaro A. Morgado*: 105, Calçada de Santo André (near Castelo de São Jorge). Tel. 87 53 95.

*Artesanato 2 Rosas*: 12, Largo Santa Cruz do Castelo (near Castelo de São Jorge), Tel. 886 24 78.

*Almorábida*: 130, Rua Senhora da Glória. Tel. 82 21 97.

### WINES (*VINHOS*)
*Macarios*: 272-276, Rua Augusta. Tel. 342 09 00.

*Caviar House*: Complexo das Amoreiras. Tel. 69 35 03.

### TAPESTRIES AND RUGS (*TAPETES E CARPETES*)
*Casa Quintão*: 30, Rua Ivens. Tel. 346 58 37.

*Alcatifas Petróleo*: Rua das Portas de Santo Antão. Tel. 347 24 43.

*Tapetes de Arraiolos Trevo*: 33, Avenida Oscar Monteiro Torres (near Campo Pequeno). Tel. 797 84 15.

*At Feira da Ladra*

### PORCELAIN (*LOUÇA DA CHINA*)
*Algifa*: 226, Rua dos Fanqueiros. Tel. 86 26 72.

*Barz e Braz*: 31-31A, Avenida de Moscavide.

*Torres & Brinkmann*: 18-22, Travessa da Trindade, Tel. 342 50 82.

### AFRICAN ART
*Tam-Tam*: 272-A, Rua da Junqueira. Tel. 362 15 86.

### SHOES (*SAPATOS*)
*Jandaia*: 76-78, Rua do Carmo/178, Rua Augusta.

*Giselle*: 231, Rua Augusta. Tel. 342 34 76. (Amoreiras branch: Tel. 69 36 54).

*Rabinos*: 29A, Avenida Roma/94, Rossio.

## Markets (*Feira*)
Fish, fresh vegetables and haberdashery are only some of the specialities sold daily at Lisbon's street-markets. You'll come across markets on your visit to the Alfama quarter, along the docks near Praça do Comércio, and in other places. These markets are particularly lively in the mornings, and most of them close in the afternoon. Lisbon's main food market is on **Mercado da Ribeira**, near the **Cais do Sodré train station**.

The city's most interesting market – the **"Thieves' Market"** (Feira da Ladra) – has been taking place since the

Middle Ages. Every Tuesday and Saturday the market is set up on **Campo de Santa Clara**, near the walls of the **São Vicente de Fora Monastery** in the eastern part of the city (see "Alfama – A Journey into the Middle Ages"). Alongside the stands of shoes and posters, hundreds of vendors display their wares: from Virgin Mary bedside-lamps and rusty screw-drivers to old bags used by the city's postmen. There are true bargains to be haggled for here. Even if you don't plan on buying anything, the Thieves' Market is well worth a visit.

The São-Pedro country market, near Sintra, takes place on the second and fourth Sunday of each month. This colorful market is the place to get home-made breads and cheeses, as well as embroidery and wood-carvings. (See Sintra in "Around Lisbon" chapter).

Near the pier, to the east of Praça do Comércio is a street-market selling imitation designer clothes, gold jewelery and more. Another quaint and colorful market on the lower part of the Rua Augusta pedes-trian mall sells masks and earings. Street performers and clowns add to the festive atmosphere here.

*For the football fans*

# Important Addresses and Phone Numbers

## EMERGENCIES

For emergency: Police, Fire Brigade, Red Cross (ambulance and first aid): Tel. 115.

British Hospital: 49, Rua Saraiva de Carvalho, Tel. 395 50 67/397 63 29.

St Luis French Hospital: 182, Luz Soriano, Tel. 347 35 81.

Red Cross Hospital: 54, Duarte Galvão, Tel. 778 30 03.

São Francisco Xavier Hospital: Estrada do Forte, Tel. 301 73 51.

Santa Maria Hospital: 7, Av. Prof. Egas. Moniz, Tel. 794 51 71.

São José Hospital: Tel. 886 01 31.

Dona Estefânia Children's Hospital: Tel. 355 82 00.

Poisoning: Tel, 795 01 43.

Blood Bank: Tel. 87 37 33.

Emergency Dental Treatment – São José Hospital: Tel. 886 01 31.

Pharmacies: Tel. 118.

Fire: Tel. 60 60 60.

Portuguese Automobile Association: Tel. 356 39 31.

## TRANSPORT AND COMMUNICATION

Bus Information: Tel. 363 93 43.

Metro Information: Tel. 355 84 57.

Train Information: Tel. 888 40 25.

Santa Apolónia Station: Tel. 86 41 81.

Cais do Sodré Station: Tel. 347 01 81.

Rossio Station: Tel. 346 50 22.

Cascais Station: Tel. 486 41 65.

Flight Departures and Arrivals: Tel. 841 67 90/841 50 00.

Central Taxi Service: Tel. 793 27 56.

Rodovíaria Nacional (RN): Tel. 54 54 39.

Telegrams:
  Tel. 183 (*CTT*).
  Tel. 182 (*Marconi*).

Telephone Information: Tel. 118

International Operator (Europe): Tel. 099.

International Operator (intercontinental): Tel. 098.

Direct Dial
  (Europe): Tel. 097;
  (intercontinental): Tel. 00.

# INDEX

# INDEX

# QUESTIONNAIRE

In our efforts to keep up with the pace and pulse of Lisbon, we kindly ask your cooperation in sharing with us any information which you may have as well as your comments. We would greatly appreciate your completing and returning the following questionnaire. Feel free to add additional pages.

Our many thanks!

To: Inbal Travel Information (1983) Ltd.
18 Hayetzira st.
Ramat Gan 52521
Israel

Name: _____

Address: _____

Occupation: _____

Date of visit: _____

Purpose of trip (vacation, business, etc.): _____

Comments/Information: _____

_____

_____

_____

_____

_____

_____

_____

**INBAL Travel Information Ltd.**
P.O.B 1870 Ramat Gan
ISRAEL 52117